# THROW IN THE VOWELS

**Rita Ann Higgins** was born in 1955 in Galway, Ireland, and still lives there. She published her first five collections with Salmon in Ireland, *Goddess & Witch* (1990), which combines *Goddess on the Mervue Bus* (1986) and *Witch in the Bushes* (1988), *Philomena's Revenge* (1992) and *Higher Purchase* (1996). Her Bloodaxe titles are *Sunny Side Plucked: Selected Poems* (1996), *An Awful Racket* (2001) and *Throw in the Vowels: New & Selected Poems* (2005).

Her plays include *Face Licker Come Home* (1991), *God of the Hatch Man* (1992), *Colie Lally Doesn't Live in a Bucket* (1993) and *Down All the Roundabouts* (1999).

She has edited *Out the Clara Road: The Offaly Anthology* and (with Gráinne Sweeney) *Word and Image: a collection of poems from Sunderland Women's Centre and Washington Bridge Centre*. In 2004 she edited *FIZZ Poetry of Resistance and Challenge*, an anthology written by young people.

She was Galway County's Writer-in-Residence in 1987, Writer in Residence at the National University of Ireland, Galway, in 1994-95, and Writer in Residence for Offaly County Council in 1998-99. In October 2000 she was Green Honors Professor at Texas Christian University. Her many awards include a Peadar O'Donnell Award in 1989 and several Arts Council bursaries. *Sunny Side Plucked* was a Poetry Book Society Recommendation. She is a member of Aosdána, and a judge of the IMPAC fiction prize in 2005.

# Rita Ann Higgins

# THROW IN
# THE VOWELS

NEW & SELECTED POEMS

BLOODAXE BOOKS

Copyright © Rita Ann Higgins
1986, 1988, 1992, 1996, 2001, 2005

ISBN: 1 85224 700 2

First published 2005 by
Bloodaxe Books Ltd,
Highgreen,
Tarset,
Northumberland NE48 1RP.

**www.bloodaxebooks.com**
For further information about Bloodaxe titles
please visit our website or write to
the above address for a catalogue.

Bloodaxe Books Ltd acknowledges
the financial assistance of
Arts Council England, North East.

Cover printing by J. Thomson Colour Printers Ltd, Glasgow.

Printed in Great Britain by
Bell & Bain Limited, Glasgow, Scotland.

*In memory of my brother Tony Higgins
who was murdered in Riyadh, Saudi Arabia,
on 3rd August 2004*

# ACKNOWLEDGEMENTS

This book includes poems selected from Rita Ann Higgins's collections *Goddess on the Mervue Bus* (1986), *Witch in the Bushes* (1988), *Philomena's Revenge* (1992) and *Higher Purchase* (1996), all published by Salmon Publishing, as well as the whole of *An Awful Racket* (Bloodaxe Books, 2001) and a collection of new poems, *Throw in the Vowels* (2005). The four Salmon collections include many more poems, and copies are still available from Salmon Publishing, Knockeven, Cliffs of Moher, Co. Clare, Ireland.

Acknowledgements are due to the editors of the following publications in which some of the new poems first appeared: *The Canadian Journal of Irish Studies, The Shop, Something Beginning with P* and *The Stinging Fly*. 'The Liberator' was commissioned by the National Council on Volunteering.

# CONTENTS

## THROW IN THE VOWELS (2005)

FROM GODDESS ON THE MERVUE BUS

(1986)

# Consumptive in the Library

About you:
You carry a kidney donor card,
not yet filled in,
a St Christopher's round your neck
on a brown shoe lace
(to ward off demons and politicians),
memories of Sweet Afton,
the racing page from the *Daily Express*
and an unsociable cough.

About me:
I carry illusions
of becoming a famous poet,
guilt about that one time in Baltinglass,
fear that the lift will stop at Limbo,
a slight touch of sciatica
plus an anthology of the Ulster poets.

Unlike your peers
you will not take warmth
from cold churches or soup kitchens,
instead, for long periods, you will
exasperate would-be poets with illusions,
in the reference room of the Galway County Library.

I started with Heaney,
you started to cough.
You coughed all the way to Ormsby,
I was on the verge of Mahon.

Daunted, I left you the Ulster Poets
to consume or cough at.

I moved to the medical section.

# Evangeline

Evangeline,
God help her,
reacts to macho men,
who in the end
expect her to survive
on the draught
of far-flung embraces,

not interested in
her food-mixer
philosophies,
her many ways
with crux pastry.

Only wanting
what she can never
give freely.

Look Evan, through
your stainless net curtains,
another far-flung embrace –
take it,

opium for the dead
self that leads
to seven second security.

She had notions,
some dreary Tuesdays,
about swish red
sports cars
and a villa
off the something
coast of France.

She saw herself
in a plunging neckline,
offering her condolences
to Anthony Quinn
Lee Marvin types.

Much later
that same lifetime,
when the kids are asleep,
she crawls out

of her apron pocket
and meets herself
for the first time that day
in the eyes of Martha Glynn,
ten *Silk Cut*
and a small white sliced.

'Will we see you
on the bingo bus
a Friday, Martha G?'

'I wouldn't miss it
for the world.'
And out of her mouth
came all the eights,
and she brought laughter
to all in Folan's shop
for the second
time this month.

# Mrs McEttigan

No coincidence was this,
it was arranged by God,
you would say.

Me, posting a letter.
You, you were just there.

You, from somewhere in Ulster,
I loved your accent.
Me, from somewhere in space,
you loved my mother.

You always said the same thing
'Your mother is in Heaven,
she was a saint, God be good to her.'

You lifted your eyes.

You, with the posh brooch,
two stones missing, your Mass hat.

I was just there.

Don't ever die, Mrs McEttigan,
I need to see you outside the Post Office
sending glances to a saint.

## Tommy's Wife

She wasn't always this bitter,
I knew her when she sang in pubs.

She was younger then and free,
a happy life she spent.

Working in Woolworths,
she kept herself well. Blue eye shadow.

She married for the sake of the kid.
A lot of envelopes she received. The day.

It started out well for her
the family stood by her then.

Tommy looks strong, many friends,
likes Guinness, sex and unemployment.

She lost blue eye-shadow first year,
Sara now five months, teething hard.

She didn't sing in pubs any more,
she wasn't as friendly as before.

The other three children didn't delay,
she remembered wearing blue eye-shadow.

The coal man hated calling now,
he didn't understand her anger.

Tommy looks strong, many friends,
likes Guinness, sex and unemployment.

## Unnecessary Work

*(for Bernie)*


Sunday evening
we walked
unwanted calories
into the prom
for leisure.

Our duty now
homeward-bound
to visit the mother's grave.

On an unkempt plot nearby
a community of pink carnations
overpowers me.

'You won't have luck for it,'
my sister said.

Later on they stood
in a black Chinese vase
accompanied by
one blooming spike
of white gladiolus
the cat had broken off.

Their agreeable essence
adds life to this room.
I mime a hurried
prayer for the repose
of the soul of
Mary Elizabeth Cooke.

## Work On

Nostalgia takes me back –
the shirt factory toilet.

Where country girls met
and sucked cigarette ends on Monday mornings.

Sunday night was discussed, the Ranch House,
his acreage, physique and the make of his car.

Precisely they swayed to and fro,
tannoy blasted sweet lyrics, their hero.

Two jived to the beat, two killed the smoke
and seven sank further into hand-basins.

Boisterous laughter echoed and betrayed lost time.
'Back to work girls,' supervisor sang.

A thousand buttonholes today.
A thousand Ranch House fantasies the weekend.

Work On.

# The Apprentices

Daily they perch
during factory lunchtimes
on their man-made Olympus.

Who will attempt to pass
through their veil of lust unscathed
by Henry Leech-along's recital
of his nine favourite adjectives?

Hardly the unprotected townie
shielded only by the active ingredients
of a lifetime's venial sins.

Maybe some young one from the Tech,
the brazen Bridget variety –
mother in a home,
father in a bottle.

Hey you! Wearers of brown acrylic pullovers,
a yellow stripe across your chest-bone
means your mother is still alive,
think not of other people's undertones,
of milk-white flesh, of touching thighs.

AnCo never trained you for this.

Stay awhile, Pavlovian pets, fill your sights
with more ambitious things,
like when your apprenticeship ends
and you are released on the world
a qualified this or that.

Right now you are an apprentice's echo,
know your station.

## Power Cut

Black-out excitement, enchanting,
chasing shadows up and down.

Delirious children play scary
monsters, the walls laugh back.

Father bear sleeps it off,
dreams of good westerns.

Mother bear thinks it cultural,
collects young, reads by candle shade.

Siblings content, maternal wing snug,
drifting softly, land of mild and honey.

Father bear slept enough, weary of culture,
'Try the lights upstairs,' he shouts.

Mother bear switches on. Another culture shock,
westerns, yoghurt and the late news.

# Poetry Doesn't Pay

People keep telling me:
Your poems, you know,
you've really got something there,
I mean really.

When the rent man calls, I go
down on my knees, and through
the conscience box I tell him,

'This is somebody speaking,
short distance, did you know
I have something here with my poems?
People keep telling me.'

'All I want is fourteen pounds
and ten pence, hold the poesy.'

'But don't you realise
I've got something here.'

If you don't come across
with fourteen pounds and ten pence soon
you'll have something at the side of the road,
made colourful by a little snow.'

'But.'

'But nothing,
you can't pay me in poems or prayers
or with your husband's jokes,
or with photographs of your children
in lucky lemon sweaters
hand-made by your dead grand aunt
who had amnesia and the croup.

'I'm from the Corporation,
what do we know or care about poesy,
much less grand amnostic dead aunts?'

'But people keep telling me.'

'They lie.'

'If you don't have fourteen pounds
and ten pence, you have nothing
but the light of the penurious moon.'

# Goddess on the Mervue Bus

Aphrodite
of the homely bungalow,
cross curtains,
off-white Anglia at the side.

Your father
(who is no Zeus)
turns old scrap
into rolled gold
nightly from memory,

looks down on you
from his scrap mountain,
hurling forks of caution
about the tin-can man

who fumbles in the aisle
of the Mervue bus,
longing for the chance
of a throwaway smile,
a discarded bus ticket.

O Goddess on the Mervue bus,
no scrap dealer fashioned
you from memory or want,
you were spun from golden
dust, a dash of dream.

Enslaver of mortals,
you choose me.

Once when you yawned
I saw myself
sitting cross-legged
on a lonely molar
waiting for the crunch.

# The German for Stomach

*(for Eva)*

I was waiting for the twenty-past
in the rain, trying to think
of the German for stomach.

While I was racking,
I took time out for
a stew fantasy.
When a blue Merc pulled
out in front of a brown Mini,
I had stew fantasy interruptus.

The man in the brown Mini
was blue and furious
but he didn't let on.
Poor Rex later that day.

The blue Merc made me think
of blue skies and blue seas,
then it came to me.
Bauch, that's it, der Bauch.
I said to myself all the way home,
except when I passed the graveyard,
time for another stew fantasy.

I got off near Kane's butchers.
Inside they were discussing
the gimp and colour of Sean Sweeney's
duodenum when the doctor opened him.
They called it the Northern Province.

It was on the tip of my tongue
and out it tumbled.
'Bauch is the German for stomach.'

His wife said,
'Are you sure you don't want
a carrier bag for that, loveen?'

I could see that
the butcher was overwhelmed,
he wanted to shout
Lapis Lazuli, Lapis Lazuli,
but instead he said,

'You wouldn't put a dog out in it.'

## Almost Communication

My father just passed me
in his Fiat 127
I was cycling my bicycle 'Hideous'.

They stopped at O'Meara's
for the *Connacht Tribune*.
As I passed I shouted
'road hog' in the window.

The occupants laughed.

Before this he owned
a Renault 12,
we called it
the 'Ballyhaunis cow killer'.

Later we met outside the sister's,
'Wouldn't you think
he'd buy you a decent bike, the miser.'

'If he had your money,' I said
and we laughed.

The neighbours with their ears
to the rose bushes
think that we're great friends.

I haven't seen his eyes for years.

# Middle-aged Irish Mothers

Germinating sopranos in conservative head squares
are the middle-aged Irish mothers in heavy plaid
coats, who loiter after Mass in churches,

    Lord make me an instrument of your peace;
    Where there is hatred, let me sow love;

to light candles for the Joes and Tommies of the drinking world,
the no-hopers, that they might pack it in,
if it's the will of God,

    Where there is injury, pardon;
    Where there is discord, union;

to pray for Susan's safe delivery, Bartley's gambling,
Mrs Murray's veins, that they would not bother her
so much, not forgetting Uncle Matt's shingles.

    Where there is doubt, faith;
    Where there is despair, hope;

Soon, not out of boredom, they will move diagonally
through their cruciform sanctuary to do the Stations
in echoing semi-song whispers,

    We adore thee O Christ we bless thee,
    because by thy cross thou hast redeemed the world;

sincere pleas to dear Jesus, that the eldest might
get off with a light sentence, pledges of no more smoking,
and guarantees of attendance at the nine Fridays,

    Where there is darkness, light;
    Where there is sadness, joy;

finally, for the Pope's intentions, Mr Glynn's brother-in-law,
the sweeps ticket that it might come up, but only if it's the will of God,
O Sacred Heart of Jesus, I place
all my trust and confidence in thee.

I like these middle-aged Irish mothers, in heavy plaid coats,
one of them birthed me on the eve of a saint's feast day,
with a little help from Jesus and his Sacred Heart.

## Ode to Rahoon Flats

O Rahoon, who made you
to break the hearts
of young girls with
pregnant dreams

of an end terrace,
crisp white clothes
lines and hire purchase
personalities?

You don't care if her
children crawl into her
curved spine,
distort her thinking.

You put Valium on a
velvet cushion
in the form of a
juicy red apple.

Rahoon, why are you
so cruel to young
husbands, hooked on
your butter voucher

bribes? If you crumbled
would it take three days
or would the ground swallow
you up, payment for your sins?

# The Long Ward

I have never seen
an old woman
eating an orange.

The long ward
for the old
and sometimes
the odd appendix.

The long ward
for craic,
for prayer,
a joke, a song
and sometimes pain.

In the long ward
Silvermints are
shared and returned
with photographs of
'My second eldest'
or 'This one is in Canada'.

Some come to visit,
to care, to love,
few to count acres
in old women's eyes.

In the long ward
it pleases when
the priest passes
your bed.

In the dead of night
a cry for somebody's son.
No welcome for the grey
box that comes to call.

Thin legs you see,
smiling mothers
in new Dunnes dressing-gowns,
new slippers,
boxes of tissues
they would never use at home.

Always one to joke
about the black doctor,
always one to complain
about the cold tea, no ham.

An eye on the clock,
a hand on the rosary beads,
pain well out of sight.

The loved grandchildren
embrace good-looking oranges
and ancient smiles.

# God-of-the-Hatch Man

*(for Community Welfare Officers everywhere)*

Smoking and yes mamming,
snoozing in the fright
of his altered expression,
caused always by the afternoon.

Tepid water sipper, coffee glutton,
pencil pointer, negative nouner,
God-of-the-hatch man, hole in the wall.

We call religiously every Thursday,
like visiting the holy well,
only this well purports to give you things
instead of taking them away.

Things like scarlatina, schizophrenia,
migraine, hisgraine but never your grain,
lockjaw and wind, silicosis,
water on the knee, hunger in the walletness.

We queue for an hour or three,
we love to do this,
our idea of pleasure,
Then whatever-past what-past he likes,
he appears.

Tepid water sipper, coffee glutton,
pencil pointer, negative nouner,
God-of-the-hatch man, hole in the wall.

He gives us money and abuse,
the money has a price,
the abuse is free.

'Are you sure your husband isn't working?'
'Are you sure grumbling granny is quite dead?'
'Are you sure you're not claiming for de Valera?'
'Are you sure you count six heads in every bed?'

Hummer of Andy Williams' tunes,
most talked about man in the waiting-room,
tapper of the pencil on the big brown desk.

God-of-the-hatch man, hole in the wall.
God-of-the-hatch man, hole in the wall.

## Mona

Mona doesn't die here
any more, she lives
in a house at the back
of her mind.

Some place small,
cosy and warm,
fully detached,
a single storey,
with no gable ending,
a high wall
but no door.

Away from
tenants' associations,
rent man's,
poor man's,
light bills,
heavy bills,
free newspapers,
and six-year-old perpetrators on skates.

When she was here
she was afraid
of salutations,
candied appreciations,
of tendon squeezing
politicians
who didn't care.

In supermarkets
she was tricked by
pennies off here,
free holidays over there,
buy three and get
anxiety for nothing.

She was a coupon saver,
she saved them
but they never saved her.

Mona doesn't die there
any more, she lives
in a shed at the back
of her house.

Some place small,
cosy and warm,
a high wall
but no door.

## Sunny Side Plucked

We met outside
the seconds chicken
van at the market.

He was very American,
I was very married.

We chatted about
the home-made marmalade
I bought two miles
from home.

He said the eggs were big,
I said he'd been eating
his carrots.

'Do you always buy
seconds chickens?'

'Only when I come late.'

The witch in me
wanted to scramble
his eggs.

The devil in him
wanted to pluck
my chicken.

We parted
with an agreement
written by the eyes.

## It's All Because We're Working-Class

*(for Michael A.)*

Through them
you could see
no rhyme reason
or gable end;
that coal bag washer
and grass eater
from the Shantalla clinic
prescribed them.

Burn your patch
he said
and be a man;
slip these on
and see into
the souls of men;
and our Ambrose
walked into
the gable end
and his life
was in splinters
thereafter.

All he really needed
was to rest his lazy eye
for a few months
and the wrong eye
would right itself.

It's like having your leg
tied behind your back
for six years
then suddenly have it released
and be told,
go now and breakdance
on a tight-rope.

It's all because we're working-class;
if we lived up in Taylor's Hill
with the coal bag washers
and grass eaters,
do you think for one minute
they would put
them big thick spy-glasses on your child?

Not a tall
not a fuckin' tall;
they'd give ya them film star glasses
with the glitter on them,
just as sure
as all their metallic purple wheelbarrows
have matching cocker spaniels
they would;

fuckin' coal bag washers
and grass eaters
the whole fuckin' lot of them;
and it's all because we're working-class.

# She Is Not Afraid of Burglars

*(for Leland B.)*

It's lunchtime
and he's training the dog again.
He says to the dog in a cross voice,
'Stay there.'
The dog obeys him.

When he goes home
he forgets to leave the cross voice
in the green where he trains his dog
and spits out unwoven troubles
that won't fit in his head.

He says to his wife,
'Stay there.'
His wife obeys him.
She sees how good he is with the dog
and how the dog obeys his cross voice.

She boasts to the locals,
'I would never be afraid of burglars
with my husband in the house.'

The locals, busting for news, ask her,
'Why would you never be afraid of burglars
with your husband in the house?'

She calls a meeting at Eyre Square
for half three that Saturday.
Standing on a chair, wiping her hands
on her apron, she explains.

'One day,' she says, in a cross voice,
'The dog disobeyed my husband
and my husband beat him across the head
with a whip made from horse hair.

That is why I am not afraid of burglars
with my husband in the house.'

# It Wasn't the Father's Fault

His father
him hit
with a baseball bat
and he was
never right since.

Some say
he was never right
anyway.

Standing
behind the kitchen table
one Sunday before Mass
his mother said,

'If Birdie Geary
hadn't brought
that cursed baseball bat
over from America,

none of this would have happened.'

# The Did-You-Come-Yets of the Western World

When he says to you:
You look so beautiful
you smell so nice –
how I've missed you –
and did you come yet?

It means nothing,
and he is smaller
than a mouse's fart.

Don't listen to him…
Go to Annaghdown Pier
with your father's rod.
Don't necessarily hold out
for the biggest one;
oftentimes the biggest ones
are the smallest in the end.

Bring them all home,
but not together.
One by one is the trick;
avoid red herrings and scandal.

Maybe you could take two
on the shortest day of the year.
Time is the cheater here
not you, so don't worry.

Many will bite the usual bait;
they will talk their slippery way
through fine clothes and expensive perfume,
fishing up your independence.

These are
the did-you-come-yets of the western world,
the feather and fin rufflers.
Pity for them they have no wisdom.

Others will bite at any bait.
Maggot, suspender, or dead worm.
Throw them to the sharks.

In time one will crawl
out from under thigh-land.
Although drowning he will say,

'Woman I am terrified, why is this house
shaking?'

And you'll know he's the one.

## Be Someone
*(for Carmel)*

For Christ's sake,
learn to type
and have something
to fall back on.

Be someone,
make something of yourself,
look at Gertrudo Ganley.

Always draw the curtains
when the lights are on.

Have nothing to do
with the Shantalla gang,
get yourself a right man
with a Humber Sceptre.

For Christ's sake
wash your neck
before going into God's house.

Learn to speak properly,
always pronounce your ings.
Never smoke on the street,
don't be caught dead
in them shameful tight slacks,

spare the butter,
economise,

and for Christ's sake
at all times,
watch your language.

## Old Soldier

He stood
at the top
of Shop Street
cursing de Valera
and he muttered
something about
the Blueshirts
and when he saw
Mrs Flanagan, he said,
'You could have
got worse than me,
but you wanted
a fisherman didn't ya?
I wasn't always
like this,' he said,
and his veins broke
and he died alone
but not lonely,
for many's the revolution
he fought in his scullery
with his newspaper
and his fine words.

# Witch in the Bushes

*(for Padraic Fiacc)*


I know a man
who tried
to eat a rock
a big rock
grey and hard,
unfriendly too.

Days later
he is still grinding,
the rock
is not getting
any smaller.

Because of this
rock in the jaw,
this impediment,
the man has become
even more angry.

No one
could look at him,
but a few
hard cases did.
They were mostly dockers;
they reckoned,

'We have seen
the savage seas
rise over our dreams,
we can look
at a bull-head
eating a rock'.

The years passed
slowly and painfully,
until one day
the rock was no more,
neither was much of the man.

He didn't
grind the rock down,
the rock
hammered a job
on him and his ego.

Then, one day
an old woman
came out of the bushes
wearing a black patch
and a questionnaire,
in her wand hand
she held a posh red pencil,
well pared.

She questioned him
between wheezes
(she had emphysema
from smoking damp tobacco
and inhaling fumes
from her open fire
in the woods)
if all that anger
for all those years
was worth it.

Old Rockie Jaw
couldn't answer
he had forgotten
the reason
and the cause.

He concluded
'Anger is OK
if you spill it,
but chewing
is assuredly
murder on the teeth.'

He had learned
his lesson
he would
pull himself together
smarten up like,
turn the other cheek,
he would go easy
on the oils that aged him.

Every now and then
he weakened,
he let the voice
from the rock take over,
an army voice
with a militant tone,

'A man is a man
and a real man
must spit feathers
when the occasion arises.'

Like all good voices
this one
had an uncle,
it was the voice
of the uncle
that bothered him,
it always
had the same warning,

'About
the witch in the bushes,'
it said,
'Watch her,
she never sleeps.'

# Anything Is Better than Emptying Bins
*(for Jessie)*

I work at the Post Office.
I hate my job,
but my father said
there was no way
I could empty bins
and stay under his roof.

So naturally,
I took a ten week
extra-mural course
on effective stamp-licking;
entitled
'More lip and less tongue.'

I was mostly unpleasant,
but always under forty
for young girls
who bought stamps with hearts
for Valentine's Day.

One day a woman asked me
could she borrow a paper-clip,
she said something about
sending a few poems away
and how a paper-clip
would make everything so much neater.

But I've met the make-my-poems-neater-type before;
give in to her once,
and she'll be back in a week asking,
'Have you got any stamps left over?'

Well I told her where to get off.
'Mrs Neater-poems,' I said,
'this is a Post Office
not a friggin' card shop,
and if you want paper-clips
you'll get a whole box full
across the street for twenty pence.'

Later when I told my father,
he replied,
'Son, it's not how I'd have handled it,
but anything is better than emptying bins.'

## Second Thoughts

It is better
not to tell
your best friend
that you have
a lover.

Because
in fourteen days
you might say
to yourself,

I should not
have told her.
Then you will go
to her house

even though
your shoes
are hurting you,
you will say to her,

my best friend,
remember
what I was telling you
fourteen days ago
at half past five,

well it's not true
I made it up
just for fun,
so forget
I ever mentioned it.

But when
you get to her house
you find
she is not in,
in fact
you find her out.

So you go
to her place of work,
she works
at the sausage factory.

People
in a small group
at the main gate say,

'She is not here
and you
can't find her in
when she is out,
you must
find her out.'

They tell you this
in a sing song way,
she has gone
to the doctor's

they say it
four times
for no reason.

You wonder
if she
has told them,
you wonder
if they
are looking at you funny
and when you pass
are they saying
to themselves,
in their
older sisters' dresses,

'There she goes
that slut,
she should be
in the sausage factory,
she should be
a sausage.'

By the time
you reach the doctor's
she has left,
you are sweating
on the road
through your clothes
into your
tight-fitting shoes.

You wonder
if keeping your secret
has made her sick
and that is why
she is at the doctor's.

You take the bus
to her house
you are there
before she opens
the front gate,

you are disappointed
when her mother tells you
through their squint window
that she has gone back to work

to make up
the time
she lost
whilst going
to the doctor's
for a prescription
for her father's
catarrh.

You decide
there and then
to take out an ad
in the local paper,

telling her
to forget all you said
that Saturday
fourteen days ago
at half past five.

She is
more than pleased;
to your face
she tells you
the next time
you meet,

she adds to this
without blinking

that you won't mind
if she goes out
with the man

you never
had the affair with
as he had been
asking her
for seven months.

And you
look round the town
you have dragged
your dirty linen through

from her house
to the sausage
to the doctor's
to the mother's

And you look up
and down the long
narrow streets
of the town you
were born in

and you wonder.

# He Fought Pigeons' Arses, Didn't He?

And she pissed
in his toilet
and ate his sausages
and he said
there was nothing
but lust between them.

And on his day off
he got an aerosol
and he wanted to spray
the arses of dead pigeons black.

And he said to her
'If it's war you want
I'll give you war.
We'll have our own war,
spraying the arses of dead pigeons black
and we'll fight seven days out of six.

And the seventh day of the six
we'll discuss the situation,
and I'll bet you
twenty black pigeons' arses
there'll still be nothing
but lust between us.'

# I Went to School with You

My children call her
Dolly Partners
and I don't check them.

Sometimes
when I'm well fed
and satisfied in every other way
and they say it,
we all laugh.

One night when I was coming home
from Mick Taylor's, half pie-eyed,
she called me.

She had no pies in her eyes
and no flies either
she spoke with her finger
her index finger,
but she never danced with the afternoon
the sunny afternoon.

lt's your duty as a mother
to control your children,'
said the finger, the index finger.
'When you are out'
('which is often,' she muttered under her manacles)
'I can hear nothing
but Madonna blaring and your youngest swearing.'

'And furthermore,' said another voice,
in an Italian accent (but we couldn't hear it)

'You miserable hag,
you never speak with your finger
your index finger,
and shame on you
you often dance with the afternoon
the sunny afternoon.
How dare you, how absolutely dare you.'

After that the finger came back on duty,
it was the index finger
and it was night duty
and it was her duty.

And the killing part of it all is, it said,

I went to school with you.

# End of a Free Ride

For years
my cousin never charged me
on the bus.

One day he said to my sister,
'Your wan would need to watch herself
stickin' up for the knackers.'

After that he went home
and had pig's cheek and cabbage,
lemon swiss roll and tea.

He called out to his wife Annie
(who was in the scullery steeping
the shank for Thursday)

'Annie love get us the milk,
was I tellin' ya,
I'll have to start chargin' my cousin
full fare from here on in.'

'Why's that?' said Annie love
returning with the milk.

'Cos she's an adult now, that's why.'

# The Tell Tattler

Have you anything
to tell us today
tell tattler?

Did you help any
old woman across
a crowded street?

Did you spread
your Sunday coat in muck
for any dainty foot?

In a pub
spacious enough
for dreamers with hope,
not near enough
to Annaghmakerrig,
you can meet the tell tattler
with a gold pelican pinned to his lapel.

Without coaxing
or pain he will tell you
about the blood he has given over the years.

He was a school teacher once.
He put streams of children into his wife,
but they fell out again uneducated and sour.

In time they shouted
from sinking Monaghan hills,
'Where is our blood-giving father now,
our chest pounder and coat spreader?
We no longer see his polished pelican
shining in the distance.

Your falling out children need to check;
that you have tells to tattle,
that you have an endless supply
of unwilling old women to drag across busy streets,
that you have cloth enough for the dainty foot,
that you have good hearing for when the bell tolls,
that you are not, our father, running out of blood.'

# Woman's Inhumanity to Woman
*(Galway Labour Exchange)*

And in this cage, ladies and gentlemen,
we have the powers that be.

Powder power,
lipstick power,
pencil power,
paper power,
cigarette in the left-hand power,
raised right of centre half-plucked eyebrow,
Cyclops power,
big tits power,
piercing eyes power,
filed witches' nails power,
I own this building power,
I own you power,
fear of the priest power,
fear of the Black 'n' Tans power.

Your father drank too much power,
your sister had a baby when she was fifteen power,
where were you last night power,
upstairs in your house is dirty power,
the state of your hotpress power,
the state of your soul power,
keep door closed power,
keep eyes closed power,
no smoking power,
money for the black babies power,
queue only here power,
sign only there power,
breathe only when I tell you power.

No pissing on the staff power,
jingle of keys power,
your brother signs and works power,
ye have a retarded child power,
you sign and work power,
look over your shoulder power,
look over your brother's shoulder power,
I know your mother's maiden name power,
look at the ground power,
I know your father's maiden name power,

spy in the sky power,
spy in the toilet power,
fart in front of a bishop power.

Apologise for your mother's colour hair power,
apologise for your father's maiden name power,
apologise for being born power.

## The Blanket Man

He calls
in his
new Volvo
collecting
the pound a week.

Him and his Volvo.

Sometimes
if she can't pay
he says,
'C'mon, c'mon missus,
if it was my stuff
I'd let you have it
for nothing.'

Leaning against
the door jamb
she doesn't
believe him.

Her and her cigarette.

# No Balls at All

The cats in Castle Park
are shameless,
they talk dirty all night long;
but not our Fluffy.

Our cat had been de-railed,
(that's Czechoslovakian for neutered)
but he doesn't know it.

He gets flashbacks
from his desire-filled past;
often along our back wall
he tiptoes tamely chasing pussy;

when he gets to the point of no return
he gets a blackout,
he well knows with his acute cat sense
that the next bit is the best bit,
but he just can't remember
what he is supposed to do.

He was an alley-cat-and-a-half once,
but felines complained,
not softly but oftenly
about his overzealous scratchy nature;
so we took him to the vet
where his desire was taken;
snapped at, whipped off, wiped out
by a man in a white coat.

It was sad really,
de-railed in body but not fully in mind;
would he ever get over it,
our cat with some desire and no equipment?

Days now
he just sits
inside our white lace curtain
envying his promiscuous alley-cat friends.

Other times,
he plays with a ball of blue wool
or a grey rubber mouse
throwing him in the air
letting on to be tough.

Still, he would have his memories,
they would come and visit him
teasing him back
to the tumbling times of testiclehood;

but sadly for the de-railed alley-cat
there is no second coming;
we came to accept it, and so did our Fluffy.

## Peter Picasso

Feeding on
potatoes and onions
and heating himself
from stolen coal
and migraine memories
of a day flush with
carrot-weight friends
and apple song,
this Protestant painter lives.

'Take out someone's appendix
make someone's teeth sing
design a hideous church,
but for the love and honour
of all that is holy
stay away from the evil easel,
that's only for the death-coloured
do-fuck-all dandified doters
who'd cut off your ear
as quick as they'd look at you.'

Peter Picasso
who could well hear
but didn't listen
let his brush take him
to this chicken shite wall world
next to Moo-hat post office,
where the crows ate the priest.
His fall is broken
and so is his heart
when an art student in tight jeans
meanders through his chicken shite world.

He conjures her up
before and after feeds
and provided it's not too wet
and she swears not to step on his wolfhound,
she can glide with him
in and out of the heads of cows
and more things less political.
And on cold winter nights
she can dance
on his stolen coal fire,
while he laughs at the walls
and checks that both ears are still there.

# Some People
*(for Eoin)*

Some people know what it's like,

to be called a cunt in front of their children
to be short for the rent
to be short for the light
to be short for school books
to wait in Community Welfare waiting-rooms full of smoke
to wait two years to have a tooth looked at
to wait another two years to have a tooth out (the same tooth)
to be half strangled by your varicose veins, but you're
198th on the list
to talk into a banana on a jobsearch scheme
to talk into a banana in a jobsearch dream
to be out of work
to be out of money
to be out of fashion
to be out of friends
to be in for the Vincent de Paul man
to be in space for the milk man
(sorry, mammy isn't in today she's gone to Mars for the weekend)
to be in Puerto Rico this week for the blanket man
to be in Puerto Rico next week for the blanket man
to be dead for the coal man
(sorry, mammy passed away in her sleep, overdose of coal
in the teapot)
to be in hospital unconscious for the rent man
(St Judes ward 4th floor)
to be second-hand
to be second-class
to be no class
to be looked down on
to be walked on
to be pissed on
to be shat on

and other people don't.

# FROM PHILOMENA'S REVENGE

(1992)

# They Believe in Clint Eastwood

In Cork prison
on Ash Wednesday
the warders have
black crosses painted
where the Cyclops
had his eye.

They believe in
the Trinity,

They believe in
reincarnation,

They believe in
dust and ashes,

They believe in
Jesus with long hair,

They believe in
Clint Eastwood,

They believe in
key consortium;

They believe in
the letter of the law.

## God Dodgers Anonymous

The Jehovah Witness
asked her
if she had a God.

No beating
around the burning bush
for this lassie.
Straight from the hip,
eyeball to eyeball job.

Have you a God?

It depends
on how you look at it,
I haven't a pot to spew libations in
yet the Gods are hopping up
all over the joint,

and funny thing
it's never
with chalice and host,
it's always
with book and pen;
sometimes a sugary grin.

'I'm God
give us four pounds
or I'll kick
your shite in.'

The Witness
witnessing a new line
in idolatry,
was flummoxed.

She told the one
who was beyond saving
to have a nice day
(she said it twice for effect).

I will, she assured,
I'll have a bastarding ball
dodging the Gods
round the grand piano
that isn't really there at all,

spitting fire
awaiting the second coming,
and when I'm not fasting for fun
I can always spend an hour or two

chewing the Moroccan sturdite binding
off the Book of Daniel
and before you can say
'Watch out for the Watchtower,'

I'll see the three horsemen of the Apocalypse
(the fourth is having a hip operation)
strutting in here, proffering
gold, frankincense and more.

## Every Second Sunday

'Can't talk now
I'm rushing up
to pay the raffle,

"The Cashel Circle"

I owe two weeks.

If I won
that hundred
no bill-boy
would get a shaggin' penny
that's for sure.

I'd buy myself
two pairs of shoes,
shop shoes,
I'd wear them

every second Sunday.'

# Him and His Terrier

The demons
made his fists dance,
no lamp-post was safe.

Before this
he was fussy about
who he said hello to.
No Eastsider would ever get
his greeting.

All his stories had
Atlantic Ocean connections;
a sailor in his heart
but he never left town.

They sought him out
for his good conversation,
it was water water everywhere.

He got worse
the stories got better
more sea, less land.
He went further away
still he never left town.

They say his brain
got sizzled with the booze.
Methylated Spirits in the end,
it stole his conversation
no more fights with lampposts.

Not fussy about Eastsiders now,
his words are few, but he repeats them.
Hello to everyone from the corner,
him and his terrier.

# Reading

To a group of prisoners
in a locked room
with a cage at the back.
It housed a warder
who lay across two chairs.

When he got restless
or peckish
he pranced up and down
in his new shoes
(they were always new
because they rarely touched ground).

'Slouched warder hears poetry
in horizontal position.'

A volunteer
made me tea,
chocolate biscuits
offered.

I read,
they listened
the one in the cage yawned
an uninterested-in-poetry yawn
(I know an uninterested-in-poetry yawn
a mile off; I interpret them).

I read some more,
a volley of questions,
some comments,
explosive laughter escaped
time and time again.

Their hunger for knowledge
stalked between lines of poems,
behind falling vowels,
in and out of hooks of question-marks
under jaded asterisks;
they wanted to know
they wanted to know.

Seconds galloped all over us
minutes ricocheted
two hours shot by,
we were all casualties.

With the jingle of keys
I was free to go
handshakes, smiles
much left unsaid,

the distance between us
several poems shorter.

I feared the man in the cage.


## Philomena's Revenge

As a teenager
she was like any other,
boys, the craic,
smoking down the backs.

Later there was talk
she broke things,
furniture and glass,
her mother's heart.

'Mad at the world,'
the old women nod
round each other's faces.

But it was more
than that
and for less
she was punished.

That weekend
she didn't leave a cup alone
every chair hit the wall,
Philomena's revenge.

Soon after
she was shifted
and given the shocks.

Round each other's faces
the old women nod,
'Treatment, treatment
they've given her the treatment.'

These days
she gets on with the furniture,
wears someone else's walk,
sees visions in glass.

She's good too
for getting the messages;
small things, bread and milk
sometimes the paper,

and closing the gate
after her father drives out,
she waits for his signal
he always shouts twice,

'Get the gate Philo,
get the gate, girl.'

# People Who Wear Cardigans Are Subversive

People who wear cardigans
are the type of people
who say,

'Would you get us
the Gold Flake
out of the cardi in the hall stand
before the race starts
like a good girl.'

People who wear cardigans are subversive.

I know a man who swore
'All popes are good.'
He was a C wearer.

They are more likely
to call their children strange names.
I knew one with a sly neck
who had a habit of saying
out of the corner of his mouth,
'J.C.B. Kellogg and Dry Bread
your tea is ready.'
He was a seven day a week C wearer.

They keep their money
and bits of granny
in biscuit tins
under the stairs.
They pray for rain
and the postponement of Christmas,
plus the evacuation of all children
to the plural of Pluto.

People who wear cardigans are subversive.

They harbour resentments against
slickless phones.

I knew a heavy breather once,
when leaving the scene
he said into the smutty night air,

'Here I am,
full of ooohs and aaahs
and the phone is jammed.'
He was a two a day C wearer.

Other C wearers
wear socks with sandals,
it goes with the territory,
'Keep the lungs
and the soles of the feet hot
and the rest will take care of itself,'
a C wearer's motto.

They get up before themselves,
get down before no one,
never shoot themselves in the foot,
but in caution
keep all loose legs under the table.

People who wear cardigans are subversive.

They wear them to hide things,
like biscuit tins,
granny bits,
rain storms,
lost Christmases,
protruding calendars,
and deep resentments.

People who wear cardigans are subversive.

Born agains and born liars
the lot of them.
One swears his grandfather could do a wheelie
while a suppressed piano
wavered on his altered ego,
he was a C wearer.

Cravat merchants
with skull rings at the gullet,
devil worshippers,
Claddagh ringers,
duffle coaters, bin lidders.

People who wear cardigans are subversive.

# Misogynist

Is the boss in?
Could he give us
a yard of a tow,

the engine's after
collapsin' on me again,
she is, the bitch.


# The Deserter

He couldn't wait
just up and died
on me.

Two hours,
two hours
I spent ironing
them shirts
and he didn't even
give me the pleasure
of dirtying them,

that's the type
of person he was,
would rather die
than please you.

But in his favour
I will say this for him,
he made a lovely corpse.
Looked better dead
than he did in our front room
before the telly,

right cock-of-the-walk
in that coffin,
head slightly tilted back
like he was going to say
'My dear people.'

He couldn't wait,
never,
like the time
before the All-Ireland
we were going to Mass,

he had to have a pint
or he'd have the gawks, he said.
That's the type he was,
talk dirty in front of any woman.

No stopping him
when he got that ulcer out,
but where did it get him?
...wax-faced above
in the morgue
that's where.

He's not giving
out to me now
for using Jeyes Fluid
on the kitchen floor,

or stuffing the cushions
with his jaded socks...
and what jaded them?
Pub crawling jaded them,
that's what.

He's tight-lipped now
about my toe separators,
before this
he would threaten them
on the hot ash.

The next time
I spend two hours
ironing shirts for him
he'll wear them.

# Questionnaire After Leaving Aillwee Cave

Does your dog bite?
(land owner, working-class,
jumped-up third generation
guttersnipe or other)

How many full stops in *The Gulag Archipelago*?

Do you wear coloured condoms?
(green, purple, gold, black or other)

Do you think Boris Yeltsin and Teresa of the Little
Flower are the same person?

Do you wear two at a time?

Do you see the humour in unemployment?

Do you believe Elvis is still alive?

Should we have free coal?

Did you have dark thoughts in the cave?

What colour should it be?

Spell Acetylsalicylic acid.

Does your wife beat you?
(yes, no, not sure)

Did you ever have impure thoughts about cheese?

Do you ride buses?

About Bree, I see mmmmmmm.
Do you believe in the power of the reflexologist?

Do all Roses of Tralee who don't make it
join the I.R.A.?
Does it hurt...no, no this is the bus question, wake up.

Do you give good phone?

Does your car own you?

Does your Credit Union own you?

Did you want to reach out
and touch someone in the cave?

Was it God?

Good.

## Light of the Moon

Question:
Can you tell me
the way to the maternity?

Answer:
Walk on a beach
in the West of Ireland
at four in the morning
in the middle of summer
with a man who's six foot two
and you'll get there
sooner or later.

Question:
Is his height the problem?

Answer:
No, the problem rises
when you stop
to look at the moon.

Question:
So is the moon
the problem?

Answer:
No, not the moon itself
but the glare from the moon
which makes you say
in seagull Russian,
'Fuse me bix foot skew
in your stocking wheat
bould you kind werribly
if I jay on the bat of my flack
for the bext three-quarters of a bour
the boon is milling me.'

Question:
And that's the answer?

Answer:
No, that's the question.
When he lies on top of you
for the next three-quarters of an hour
shielding you from the light of the moon
the answer comes to you.

Question:
Like a flash?

Answer.
No, like the thundering tide.

# Cloud Talker

Two men
are putting a roof
on the neighbour's shed.

They are both tall
very tall,
they look alike
very alike,
they would pass for brothers,
they would pass.

One hardly acknowledges her
(in fact for no bad reason
they don't anything each other).

The other one makes cloud talk.

She spies on them
from behind the net curtain
where she flushes out
stale and ancient tea-leaf schemes
from two breakfast cups.

This day without charity,
when she is pegging down
their aggressive sheets,
she says to cloud talker,

'I love a man
as tall as you,
as fair as you,
as blue-eyed as you,
but I can't put my hands
inside his shirt
because he's doing life.'

Just then
no-bad-reason spoke.

'Twin brother,' he said,
'enough of your talk,
you'll bring on the rain.
Throw me that hammer,
let's get on with the nails.

We've already been here
half a lifetime.'

## Old Timers

She loves the clockman;
she leans on his shoulder
from her bicycle,
cycling slowly
through a field.

Slightly out of step,
the botched hip job
leaves him
one foot shorter
than the other.

She adores him;
his slight tick-over
his offbeat with time
but never with her heart.

Children have worn a path
for these older lovers,
harmony not always seen,
the eye is good
but the heart is better.

They're heading for the pub now.
She loves the clockman;
she leans on his shoulder
from her bicycle.

On their return,
his short step less noticeable,
harmony more visible
as the falling together starts.

The treasured bicycle
now takes third place;
it trails like an unwanted relative,
uncle somebody.

When they hit home
he'll make the tea,
he'll rub her old feet,
they'll make yes and no sentences
for ages with love,

and if the voice is good
she'll sing out to her clockman
sweet youthful melodies,

making him forget
years, months, days,
minutes, seconds,
ticks, tocks,

until the only down-to-earth sound
is the click of her new teeth
as she whispers, gently,

'Love, oh love,
there's no time like the present.'

## His Shoulder-blades and Rome

*(for Pat Arthurs)*


The prisoner
in one of the cells
on the 4's landing
just under the roof,

can hear the soldiers
jumping up and down
trying to keep warm.

The prisoner
lying back in his bed
is thinking about
his ex-wife Maria
(once the sunshine of his life),

about the time
he took her on holiday
to the Costa del Sol,
and how they separated
two weeks later.

It's getting colder,
colder than cold.
The soldiers are jumping
non-stop now;
they are freezing.

They are interrupting
his thoughts
about Maria, his ex-wife
(once the sunshine),

about the time
he took her on holidays to the Costa,

where she blew non-stop kisses
between his shoulder blades and Rome
easing the sting of yesterday's sun.

# Butter Balls

Mountains of butter voucher recipients
met outside the meat hall
in Mill Street,
to hear misery guts
most miserable minister of miseries
spill the mean beans
about the extension
of the butter voucher scheme.

Oh mean miserable minister
misser of minor misdemeanours
and moving trains,
side tracker,
dirty talker,
spiller of misery,
and mean beans,
extender of butter voucher schemes,
tell us the miserable news.

'Good morning mealies,
it gives me great pleasure
(butter pleasure)
to tell all of you
who met today
outside the meat hall
in Mill Street,
which I nearly missed
owing to a minor misdemeanour,

that I oh miserablist of miseries
have made a meanagerial decision
for your benefit,
I've decided to extend
the butter voucher scheme
for another two years,

P.S. and et cetera.
It gives me minister of most miseries
ever more pleasure
(butter pleasure)
to tell you recipients
of unsocial smellfare,

that the above mentioned
butter voucher or B.V.
as we say at the MTs
has been increased from
54p to 55p per V.'


## Dead Dogs and Nations

*(for Anne Kennedy)*


Other things upset her most
like dead dogs and nations.
Take the Gulf War,
she cried for every side,
it took her over
completely and without mercy.

Night, noon
and every phone call
she was Gulf grieving.

Once at a bus stop
she was overheard saying,
'They're killing my people.'

Her compassion immense;
her heart broke for
dead dogs and nations.

Her family
she cut out
at the greeting card stage,
one happy birthday to you
too many in a long line
of smiling faces
turned her off
she disowned the lot,
right down to the cooing babies

in Matinee coats and white souls.
These baby beauties
who brought out the best in others
did nothing for her.

Once she said out loud,
'Purgatory O Purgatory'
no one knew what she meant.

She didn't believe in innocence
or the power of prayer,
Popes and politicians could sizzle.

She went on caring
for dead dogs and other nations
she over-cared, she over-loved
but not really;

her own backyard
was a dark balloon
full of snakes and razor blades.

It's not that the grass
was always greener,
just it was always
under someone else's foot.

When Kelly's dog died
she broke for good.

# I'll Have to Stop Thinking About Sex

*(for Tadgh Foley)*

People
are beginning
to notice.

Take
the two wans
at the market,
the fish market.

They looked
at each other
then they looked
at me.

Then
one said
to the other,

'Other,
that woman
is holding the French loaf
like it was a fisherman.'

They thought
that I thought
that the French loaf
was a you know what.

But they were wrong
'You know whats'
are often hard to fathom,

fishermen are fishermen
(spongy as earlobes).

The French loaf
was fresh and hot,

the only way
to hold it,
a reasonable way
to cool it.

They were wrong
the two wans,
with their know-your-loaf
philosophies
their all-seeing eyes
their all-fish tales.

## Between Them

You only see
good-looking couples
out driving
on a Sunday afternoon.

His hair is blonde,
her eyes are blue.

Between them
they have no broken veins
stretch marks
Guinness guts
fat necks
barrel chests
or swollen ankles.

Between them
they never curse.
His give-away sign
is the way he holds the steering wheel
in the twenty-to-two position.

Her give-away sign
is the sweep of the perfume
she leaves lingering at the traffic lights
where the pedestrians often turn green.

Between them
they never eat fries
red or brown sauce
shanks of anybody
mackerel from the basin.

Putrid, they say, putrid.

Between them
they have no cholesterol in the blood
no coal in the shed,
everything is centrally heated,
it's easier that way
cuts out the middle man
and the mess.
Sometimes
when they are not out
looking good-looking,

between them
you could fit:
two McInerney Homes
three Berlin Walls
Martha Glynn's fantasies
four empty factories (I.D.A.)
seventeen rocket couriers (slightly overweight)
forty-eight good quality reconditioned colour TVs
incalculable curriculum Vs

cat fights
frog fights
bull fights
dog fights
broken hearts
hearts in jars
lost wars
lost teeth
teeth in jars
Pope's intentions
sexist free Bibles
Ceaucescu's wealth
Bush's blushes
tea-leaf prophecy classes
sole-of-the-feet prophecy classes
black-eye prophecy classes
white-of-the-eye prophecy classes
moveable feasts
grow your own cameras
poster poems
dirty water
and murder mysteries.

## He Leaves the Ironing-board Open

He likes
crisp white shirts
and Tracey Chapman.
He leaves
the ironing-board open
in his mobile home
near the motorway,
so that he is halfway there
if he ever makes the decision
to go out.

He plays
Tracey Chapman
really loud
in his mobile home
near the motorway,
so that he can't hear
the noise of the cars
or the screech of his loneliness
crashing into him
from every side.

# Space Invader

*(for Louise Hermana)*

Hey Missus,
you're the poet,
write a poem
about me,

about the time
I lived
in a toilet
for six months,
no shit girlie.

Nothing to whine
home about
but it was dry
and beggars
can't be choosers.

You're the poet,
the one with
the fancy words,

I'm the one
with the toilet –
they call me
the space invader.

A toilet, a toilet
my kingdom
is a toilet –
give us a poem
or piss off missus.

I'm livin'
on twisted pennies
now,
but not for long,

Christmas
is up
round Moon's corner,
and I'll soon
be livin'
off the hog.

I've an uncle
a docker
full card and all
says there's money
in dirty coal yet,

and the coal boat
has a leak,
know what I mean
girlie missus.

Write a poem
about me
about the time
I lived
in a toilet
for six months.

After all
you're the poet
girlie missus
the one with
the fancy words.

## It's Platonic

Platonic my eye,

I yearn
for the fullness
of your tongue
making me
burst forth
pleasure after pleasure
after dark,

soaking all my dreams.

# Limits

There were limits
to what he could take
so he took limits,
sometimes he went
over the limits,

other times the limits
went over him,
not in any aggressive way
down the neck way
oil the oesophagus way,

cool and refreshing
on a hot summer's day way;
so he had a problem
he had to watch it.

His mother said it
so did his wife, watch it
the wise ones said, watch it.

But sometimes
when he wasn't looking
limits got him
handcuffed him
forced him into it,
down the neck way
oil the oesophagus way,

when he was
over the limits
nobody wanted him,
he was an unwashed, unwanted,
unwilling, unattractive,
over the limits slob.

He never got wise
he only got older,
the limits got higher
the climb got harder.
He reached nowhere
in jigtime,
anywhere in no time.

He had no limits
no fun, no jokes
no-how, no jumpers

only sitters
who sat around with him
and blamed the grass for growing,
the Government, the I.R.A,
the A.B.C, the I.U.D,
the U.F.O, the I.T.V.
He was a paid up member
of the sitters and blamers gang.

After a while
he had no need
to watch it,
limits now looked
for plump ones
half his measure
who still had fight.

He had fought
all his battles
and lost.
He was a lost limit
a limitless loss,

a winner only
when his pockets
were full
and his jokes were new.

Who was he now
at thirty-five –
a limited old man
who hadn't lived;
lingering on street corners,
searching for
shoot-the-breeze friendships
without commitments
or frontiers.

# Rat-like Dogs and Tattooed Men

*(for Cathy Lafarge)*


In Creepy Crawley
in West Sussex
big men with tattoos
walk rat-like dogs
into pubs.

When the rat-likes
go for the ankle bone
you are told
'Wouldn't touch you.'
Another says,
'He'd lick you to death.'

These big men,
one with his elbow
on his knee,
bellow down the ear
of your friend,

'He's a pisser,
pisses everywhere,
but I'll knock it
out of him,

a few round the head
and he'll sit up.'

You try not to look
at his tattoos
but you can't help it,
they're everywhere,
even on his lips.

'That one's a snake,'
he says,
'an anaconda
could eat elephant eggs
and spit out the shells,
could wrap himself
round the belly of an ass
and strangle it.'

Later, and glad to be home
the whole scene
dances in my head.

I question nothing
but the elephant eggs.

## If You Want to Get Closer to God

A young one like you
shouldn't be left
on your own to wither,
not with the likes
of Kill Cassidy
knocking around.

He'd knock a son
out of you no problem,
no better man,
and he wouldn't even
work up a sweat.

Don't know what
the world's coming to
at all at all.
In Carraroe
they're swopping keys.

God will get
the upper hand yet,
they'll all end up
filling holes in the road
with their sins,
and their Jezebel shoes.

The Claddagh church
is my favourite
there's a lovely one
of the Virgin there
a right beauty,

they say the sculptor
hit ecstasy
before he finished
the five sorrows,

seven hours the ecstasy lasted
down on one knee, mouth open
chisel in the writing home position.

Badly off,
Bad-mouth Keogh
said it was no ecstasy
when he saw the bone setter
trotting on his jaw the next day.

Yeah, the Kill Cassidy's
the boy for you,
he'll knock a son all right
as many sons as you like
no better man,

I'm not mad about
the new Cathedral myself
too many frills for my liking,
keep it simple is my motto.
If you really want to get closer to God
Knock Shrine's your man,
no frills, no fuss
stark reality,
plenty of wheelchairs
plenty of buses.

# New York

The Korean
who runs a flower shop
in Brooklyn says,

'Every day
people come in here
and steal from me.

They say,
when they are edging out
with my flower basket,

C'mon c'mon man
my wife just had four babies,
what can I tell you
I look at her
she gets pregnant.

Try taking this from me man
and for your trouble
I'll give you a bullet
in the head.

Although
all Koreans love a song,
I never say,
Have a nice day
I always say,
Take the flowers.'

## H-Block Shuttle

*(for L. McKeown)*

We see nothing
from the Inter-Kesh-Shuttle
the H-mobile,
only the people seated
on the other side
(and no one really knows
what side they are on).

Somewhere between H's,
an overdue light bill,
thoughts of a holiday for two
(in anywhere but Gibraltar)
and the one who's doing life,

the H-mobile stops,
we wait for the doors to open
Tic toc, tic toc, tic toc.

Time for a head count.
He counts our heads
on his fingers
for a living,
while the people seated here
count the relatives
they have left
(some are running
out of uncles).
Some brazen it
with a false laugh,
some stare ahead
forgetting to blink.

A woman whispers
'We're going to the showers,'
others throw Mass card glances
at their shoes
(with them he counts
the back of their heads).

'Hey mister,
what do you do
for a shilling,
a queen's shilling?'

'I count heads
for a living,
my clean living.'

'Do you speak
to the heads
that you count?'

'I'm not paid
to speak to the heads
who don't count.

I'm paid to count
the heads who don't speak.'
'And why
do the heads
that you count
not speak?'

'Outside the dogs bark
to ensure
that the heads
who don't count
that I count
don't speak...'

'And what about
the no-windows scare?'

'No windows are there
to ensure
that the heads
who don't count
that I count
don't see.'

'And what is
it out there
that the heads
who you count
shouldn't see?'

'I count heads
on my fingers
for a living,
for my clean living,
for my queen's shilling.

I get paid
to count heads
who don't count,
not to tell you

what the heads
who don't count
that I count
shouldn't see.'

We see nothing
from the Inter-Kesh-Shuttle,
the H-mobile,
only the people seated
on the other side
(and no one really knows
what side they are on).

# Trapped Doctor on Cork to Galway Bus

He was on the Connemara run
for years,
twelve pins, twelve bins,
he knew them all.

He grew tired
of the mountains
and the sheep.

He longed for the sight
of a field of grass,
nothing to write home about,
just a square field
an honest field
level and unpretentious.

He'd still take it
with a cow in it
maybe an old bath
a few rusty gates for a fence,
no sheep or mountains need apply.

He always said
there was a trapped doctor inside him
'One day I'll go back to college'
was his swan song.
Back to Cork
was as far as he got;
it's a long way
depending on how you walk it.

One day
on the Cork to Galway
on the hottest day of the year,
while we sizzled,
a draught fantasiser asked him,
could he open the door please.
He said it was against regulations.

That night
when he made love
to his wife,
he said,

'Gloria love, Gloria,
let on I'm tall.'

# The Power of Prayer

*I liked the way*
*my mother*
*got off her bike*
*to the side*
*while the bike*
*was still moving,*
*graceful as a bird.*

We watched out for her
after Benediction.
It was a game –
who saw her head-scarf first,
I nearly always won.

The day the youngest
drank paraffin oil
we didn't know what to do.

All goofed round the gable end,
we watched, we waited,
head-scarf over the hill.

Knowing there was something wrong
she threw the bike down
and ran.

She cleared fences
with the ailing child,
Mrs Burke gave a spoon of jam,
the child was saved.
Marched indoors
we feared the worst,
our mother knew
what the problem was.

'Not enough prayers
are being said in this house.'

While the paraffin child
bounced in her cot
we prayed and prayed.

We did the Creed,
a blast of the Beatitudes
the black fast was mentioned,

the Confiteor was said
like it was never said before,
Marie Goretti was called
so was Martha,
we climaxed on the Magnificat.
After that it was all personal stuff.

*I liked the way*
*my mother*
*got off her bike*
*to the side*
*while the bike*
*was still moving,*
*graceful as a bird.*

For good neighbours with jam
for Pope's intentions
for God's holy will
for the something of saints
the forgiveness of sins
for the conversion of Russia
for Doctor Noel Browne
for the lads in the Congo
for everyone in Biafra
for Uncle Andy's crazy bowel
for ingrown toenails
and above all
for the grace of a happy death.

# Jackdaw Jaundice

When the geezer
on the bridge
near Heuston Station
asked the nun
for the price
of a cup of tea,

her answer was in
the hooves from hell sounds
she made with her heels.

He replied in winegorian chant,

'Typical jackdaw jaundice,
clip–clopitty–clop
and a black sail away.'

# I Want to Make Love to Kim Basinger

I'm terrified
of hairdressers
who always say
Are you going
to the dance
tonight love?

I always say yes
even though
I'm never going
to the dance
tonight love.

They say the dance
I say the dance
we all say the dance
we say, the dance.

They think
I should be going
to the dance
and what they think goes.

I always
have my hair done
so I can look good
in the bath
in case
Kim Basinger
calls round.

If she takes the trouble
to climb four flights,
the lift isn't there
so it doesn't work,
and if she takes
the further trouble
of five lefts,
two rights
and three straight aheads,
I want to be ready for her.

I never told them this
at the hairdressers,
I always say dance dance,
I'm going to the dance.

It pleases them,
they go from there
they spread the web
cast the nets
they get to the root,
before I know it
I'm on the Persian carpet.

One called Consumpta consumes,
she talks in scrunch and blow dry
kiss curl mousse or gel
bee-hive-jive, French plait
Afro comb all alone.

With her, everyone is my woman;
my woman this, my woman that
my woman with the highlights
my woman with the perm
my woman with the worm.

When consuming Consumpta says
did you just have a baby,
your hair is falling
into your tea.
I always say yes
I start to shout,
I say yes Consumpta yes.

Give her anything
but split ends.
She says,
give me anything
but split ends.

No split ender
ever shifted
the bull of the ball
and we do want
the bull of the ball
don't we
otherwise why bother

getting our hair done
in the first place,
then she says Spanish,
she says Comprendo.
I say yes Consumpta yes.
Once after shouting
over her shoulder
to other, as yet,
less Consuming Consumptas;
Remind me I owe the till three pounds,
she looked me in the eye,
through the mirror,
and said,

hot oil that's it,
hot oil
is the jigger you need.
Steeped in it
for twenty
you'll come out
a new woman,
you'll taste your tea then
and it won't be wearing a moustache,
mark my words.

And dance, dance
don't talk to me
about dance,
you'll be dancing
that much,
they'll be seeing
sparks off your nipples,

hot oil, that's it
the jigger you need,

hot oil today
the bull of the ball tonight.
Mark my words.

FROM HIGHER PURCHASE
(1996)

# The Flogger

*A man with such a belly*
*can never ever become a flogger*
KAFKA: The Trial

He wanted to be a flogger –
not just any old
swing the taws
Tom-Jack run-o'-the-mill flogger
he wanted to be
the best flogger in town.

His father, a fines administrator
his mother, a fine administrator's wife
he knew about the letter of the law.

He longed to flog.
He would flog miserable souls
to within an inch of their miserable lives.

He fancied they would go away galled –
but confident that they were flogged,
not by any Jack-Tom chancer flogger.

They would respond to
how's she cutting greetings,
'flogged' they'd say,
'not by any run-o'-the-chancer flogger
by the foulest flogger in town,
and furthermore it was a Double
Special Offer Monday flogging
me and the wife together
me with the left hand
the wife with the right hand
our agonies complete.'

When the town flogger
sullied his career
by blind dating a one-time flogged soul,
the fines administrator's son
took the reins.

The slim back
was his favourite
the back to tear a shirt from
the cat-o'-nines-delight.

But this flogger,
not just any
swing the mill
run-Jack-over-Tom flogger
was a very fair flogger.

He always gave the choice
'take it off or have it torn off,'
that won him acclaim
that, and his Special Offer Mondays.

Like every good flogger
he had his faults,
he had five stomachs
he had to keep them filled
he dipped often into other people's pots.

Eventually he got caught,
his father, a fines administrator
his mother, a fine administrator's wife.
The flogger, the fair old flogger
the 'take it off or have it torn off' flogger
got fifty lashes
inferior lashes by his standards,
the shame of the flogger
being flogged left its mark,
especially when he met
souls he had flogged
and flogged well,
his shame left him smaller
and red all over.

# He Could Get Radio Prague

When he said
he could get
an oil rig for scrap
just like that,

and that
he could get
Radio Prague
on his transistor,

and that
he never backed horses
each way or in a placepot
only on the nose
always on the nose,

and that
he knew rakes of really famous actors
because of all the films
he was extra in,

and that
he was only hangin' round here
until Peter, their Peter,
came over from Canada with the jingle,

and that
it wouldn't bother him one bit
if he never saw
this fuck arse of a town ever again,

no one at the bus stop anythinged him.

# He Is Not Thinking About Last Night

He is sitting
on a bollard
his head in his hands –
rats and ladders
from liqui-land
hoping for
a lift to town.

Cars are passing him goodo.
He is thinking into his hands
'How am I going to get a lift to town
for the cure, Jesus Mercy Mary help.'

He wasn't even out last night
he was in with M spirit Esquire
gut rotter
cell begrudger
brain emptier
usher to oblivion.

He head-in-the-handed it so long
there was talk of a plaque,
mind you it was only small talk.

The dissenters say he dogged it
and no plaque should he get,
they said he should be plaqueless.

They had a main speaker
who shouted from the back
of a rejuvenated Hillman Imp.
At times they joined in.

Usually the main speaker let rip
'Plaque what plaque, plaque my eye,
did they give me a plaque
when I got cancer of the ear lobe
and my ear fell off,

not on your ninny,
cop yourself ons they gave me
and plenty of them.

Haven't you got another ear they shouted
listen more carefully
with the one you've got
and you might be better off,
some things aren't worth hearing
some things are better left unsaid
that's the type of plaque I got.'

In time the plaque went up
and as plaques go this one didn't
weather beaten it stayed like himself
long after hours and hours.

Still the cars never stopped
but they slowed to a crawl.
Usually the eldest would do the honours
unless the eldest was insane
or under the throes of botulism,
then it would fall to the second eldest.

Males had superiority on Sundays,
Tuesdays and every third Saturday
all other days females read first,
except when the interlopers
tried to get a piece of the action.

Then the townies
even the dissenters
would take on plaque pride.

A deep breath was taken first;
these are the very boyos
who said earlier
'plaque what plaque, plaque my eye',

now they are telling the interlopers
'if any plaque needs readin' aloud
in this town
we have the vehicles
and the voice power
so feck off to Loughrea, Lockjaw
or Monaghan town for yourselves'.

So this day, a Sunday,
the plaque was read
the vehicle, a rejuvenated Hillman Imp

the occupant, a show-off
wearing one ear and beaming
with plaque pride
(the interlopers were balking in the bushes),

'This man is not thinking about last night
night of passion how good it wasn't,
he is hoping one of you family albums
with the lattice vests
the gaudy shades
the tattoos,
will stop your tripod philosophies
your umbrella loins
your barium meals
your poxy cars
and give him a lift to town
for the cure Jesus Mercy Mary help,

before his
soap-box eyes
challenge onto his palms
tour guide up his sleeves
slip-jig round his wind pipe
hammer down the town without him and jive.'

# Donna Laura

Petrarch you louser,
I'm here plagued with the plague
and you're off chasing
scab free thighs.

Milli is the only one
who stood by me,
not that you could say stood,
she blesses herself
a thousand times a day
her head always ground-ward bound
prayers and half prayers
tripping her as she goes.

She scalds the arse off me
with the hot bricks
she keeps pushing between the sheets.

Between the shivers
the high fevers
and the hot bricks
I'm beside myself with anxiety.

Francesco, remember that Good Friday
in the church of Santa Chiara?
You nearly knocked a column
gazing at me
plague free at the time
I had hardly a pimple.

*Milli, off your knees,*
*and fetch me that ointment and gauze*
*wet my lips while you're at it.*

It was Easter before
we met again
those three days
like three lifetimes,

little did I know
that the sonnets
were oozing out of you
and little Madonna Laura
was sparking them off.

*Milli don't forget*
*to wrap a clean rag*
*around my chin when I go*
*give up that snivelling*
*and keep them Aves to yourself.*

Whenever there was
a whiff of Pope in the background
you no longer saw me
only chalices, gold embroidered cloaks
large tracts of land
and Bulls, loads of Papal Bulls.

O Petrarch, you poser,
you were always swaggering
in and out of the Papal courts.

As for the sonnets
you were seen tearing them up
and throwing them petal-like
around the marketplace,
the Pope thought your piss was lemonade.

Petrarch, may you get what I have,
whoever rolled back that stone
should have rolled it over your head.

## Higher Purchase

We saw them take
her furniture out,

the new stuff
her kids boasted about
six months before.

The Chesterfield Suite
the pine table and chairs
the posh lamp
the phone table,
though they had no phone.

When it was going in
we watched with envy
she told her kids out loud
'You're as good as anyone else
on this street'.

When it was coming out
no one said anything,
only one young skut
who knew no better, shouted,

'Where will ye put the phone now,
when it comes?'

# When the Big Boys Pulled Out

In S.P.S.
we parted the nuts
we parted the washers
between this and lunch time
we smoked.

A nut in this barrel
a washer in that barrel
never a washer in with a nut
never a nut with a washer be.

After lunch
was much the same,
divide and conquer
nut and washer
no thought for cancer
we all smoked on.

We had plenty of
nut and washer jokes
but they were all played out
and only used
when a new girl started.

We were cruel
sending her for a glass hammer,
a bucket of compressed air.
Soon enough she was flashing the ash,
and goading us on an all-out strike,
when we got dermatitis.

This decisive thinker won us over
in a hurry, making her part
of our nut and washer brigade.

Our fag breaks
became our summer holidays
when the Big Boys pulled out.

Now everything
was in the one barrel
butts, nuts, bolts,
washers, dryers
eye shadows

wedding dresses
bell-bottoms
hopes, dreams, fantasies
platforms,
Beatlemania,

Costa del Sols
where-will-you-get-work-now jokes
that were no jokes
Benidorums
all alore-ums.

Our fag breaks
became our summer holidays
when the Big Boys pulled out.
No further need
of our discretion
a nut here
a washer there.

# The Flute Girl's Dialogue

Plato, come out now
with your sunburnt legs on ya
don't tell me to play to myself
or to the other women.

'Discourse in Praise of Love' indeed.

Bad mannered lot,
even if I cough when I come into the room
it does not stop your bleating.
That couch over there seats two comfortably
yet every time I enter
there's four of you on it
acting the maggot
then if Socrates walks in,
the way you all suck up to him.

Small wonder Plato
you have a leg to stand on
after all the red herrings
you put in people's mouths.
You hide behind Eryximachus
and suspend me like tired tattle.

'Tell the Flute Girl to go' indeed.

Let me tell you Big Sandals
the Flute Girl's had it.
When I get the sisters in here
we are going to sit on the lot of you,
come out then gushing platonic.

The Flute Girl knows
the fall of toga tune
the flick of tongue
salt-dip hemlock-sip
eye to the sky tune
hand on the thigh tune
moan and whimper talk
dual distemper talk.

When you played I listened,
when I play, prick up your ears.

# The Trouble With Karen Reilly

She is mirror mirror
she is too much eye-liner
she is lipstick redder than blood
she is Jon Bon Jovi
she is the salt.

Her skirt's
way too short
her jumper's
way too low
and cheek
she could fire it
faster than lead.

If anyone called
she was ready,
she was always ready
set and she went
for spills and thrills

down the Falls
in a stolen car
a back seat passenger
with non-stop gossip
of the weekend disco
who shifted who
who got the ride

she laughed for nothing
she sang for a hoot
'Everything I do
I do it for you.'

She was wild
she was free
she was Bon Jovi,

with the bullet in her back
she was Clegged.

# Mothercare

The girls came over
to see the new buggy,
the rainbow buggy,
the sunshine stripes.

O.K. it was expensive
but it was the best
and welfare pitched in.

It had everything –
she listed its finer points,
underbelly things we hadn't seen.

A little touch here
and it collapses
a little touch there
and it's up like a shot,
you barely touch this –
and you're in another street
another town.

A mind of its own
a body like a rocket
it's yours to control –
just like that.

She swears she'll keep it well
immaculate, she says, immaculate.

When she's nearly eighteen
it will still be new,
Tomma-Lee will be two and a half,

she can sell it then
and fetch a high price,

almost as much as she paid.

# The Quarrel

Zeus, loveen,
help me, help my son
who runs rings around me,
but not for long.

That rotten cur Agamemnon
has stolen his prize
and you know the way
our family gets about prizes.

Remember that time
we won the two turkeys at bingo,
they all said it was a fix
and I threatened to bring up
every last crab from the deep
to piss on their cabbage.

And you, you know all,
must know how I have defended you
against that Shantalla crowd
who call you The Bonking Swan
behind your lovely back.

Bow your head,
loving know all,
let everyone see the sign.
Show them die-hards
my invitation
didn't say don't come.

When Zeus bowed
his holy head
the heavens shook,
swans all over Sligo
were taking oaths
and cover, much cover.

Hera wasn't one bit pleased
'I see slithery feet was here,
begging as usual,
what did she want this time –
to plait your sable brows?'

Zeus tried to interrupt.

'Didn't I see her
with my own ox-eye
wrapped around your knees.

Fine thing
in my own house.
I can't glide into the kitchen
and have a cup of tea
and a kit-kat
but old slithery feet
has my tiles ruined,
well I'm fed up with it, by jingo.'

Just then Hephaestus appeared,
sick as a gone-off mackerel
that the dinner would be spoiled
with all the quarrelling.
(Zeus nipped out for a solpadeine)
'Mother,' he said
'never mind that Barry's tea
drink this and swallow your resentments
you can't win against Zeus.

One time for nothing
he caught me by the foot
and hurled me into
the middle of next year
I'm still dizzy and lame.'

Hera laughed at this.
Apollo, mad to get
on *The Late Late Show*,
took out his harp, by Jove,
and they all drank nectar
till the bulls came home
and the craic was mighty
and Hera forgetting her jingo
let Thetis slide easy into the sea.

# Whiplashed

My client, your honour,
is experiencing great difficulty
sitting from a standing position
and standing from a sitting position.

His pelvic spring
is not what it used to be,
in fact on the night in question
his pelvic spring sprung.

His left trapezius muscle is trapped
and is starting to make encores
half two degrees south of his right hippus,
this carry-on is involuntary.

Any examination of the throacic spine
activates the voice box,
and my client keeps repeating
in a sirloin staccato,

*Your numbskull killed a swan*
*with my new numberella.*

Since the whiplash
my client is left-handed.
This makes shoe removing very difficult,
especially if you're in Dublin
and your shoes are in Cork.

Another thing, your honour,
since the lash
my client is unable to –
how shall we put it – flatuate.
This unfortunate condition
is causing a false fullness
which my client erogenously believes
will only be relieved
by forty lumber punctures.

Have you any idea, your honour,
the cost of a lumber puncture nowadays?

I implore your honour,
in your decision for compensation,

to think long and hard
about pelvic springing
which is still negative
despite 140 calls to
Orgasmic Orla
on the 'Let's Talk Dirty' line.

My client reminds me, your honour,
that before this pelvic punishment,
he was cock of the walk.

## Remapping the Borders

In Texas
after the conference
they put on a céilí,
nearly everyone danced,
a few of us Margarita'd.

In jig time
everyone knew everyone.
After the Siege of Ennis
a woman asked me,
'Could you see my stocking belt
as I did the swing?'

I was taken aback.

Me, thigh, knee, no,
I saw nothing.
I saw no knee
no luscious thigh
no slither belt,
with lace embroidered border
that was hardly a border at all.

I was looking for the worm in my glass.

I thought about her after,
when I was high above St Louis.
I'm glad I didn't see
her silk white thighs
her red satin suspender belt
with black embroidered border
that was hardly a border at all.

I swear to you
I saw nothing,
not even the worm
lying on his back
waiting to penetrate my tongue.

# Mamorexia

You should be
down on your knees
thanking God
with the lovely
husband ya have.

Look at Beatrice Cohen
the teeth nearly rotten
in her head –
what chance has she?

And her sister
spitting out babies
every time she coughs
and none of them
havin' any fathers,
except that lad
with the dark skin.

She was told often enough
no good would come of her
swanking round the docks
in those sling backs.

Lookit you
with those two angels
with them lovely
white bobby socks on them
and their father's eyes.

Cop yourself on –
your shadow looks
better than ya,
pull yourself together
and for crying out loud
go and eat something

something decent.

## The Winner

It was his dog
you could tell the way
it clung round his neck
like a collar.

The remote control was his
his name was etched
with a broken penknife
across the top – His.

He always got
the biggest chop
when he was eating,
the biggest chop
he said, down boy down.

He spent all day every
burping and channel surfing
with his own ensignified remote control.

He was in Minnesota once
to check the time.
He always said,
'When I was in Minnesota
the chops were much bigger.'
He said it every day
chops, Minnesota, bigger.

His wife wished
and wished
that he would
go to Minnesota
and stick to
the biggest chop
and check the time.

He wasn't into divorce
or dirty dish washing,
he stayed and stayed
with his dog collar
his remote control
his greasy chop.

Got to hand it to him
on that remote control
he was fast,
he couldn't be beaten
he channel surfed all day,

at night he always came first.


## The Taxi Man Knows

I see them going off there
and hardly a stitch on them
one young thing
I swear to God
you could see her cheeks
another lassie
you could see her tonsils,

and they come home then
crying over spilt milk

if she was my daughter
I'd give her something to cry over.

# When it Comes to the Crutch

Most of Joy-Roy-Gang
end up on crutches,
some die all of a sudden
some die all of the time
others join the Joy-Roy-Groupies Club,
they have afternoon crutch races.
Better than snatching
where the buzz is only part-time.

Hard chaws anyway
(look at Elvis Kelly
got a hook caught in his flesh
nearly lost his primer).
If you're on crutches
you're doubly hard.
So it is written on the fag wall:
*Two legs good*
*Two legs with sticks gooder.*

At the crutch race
this guy is hot, shit hot
hops like a pro, a real pro
he nearly always wins,
he jibes the others,

'Sissies, step-in-the-hallas
couldn't catch a wan-winged butterfly
with asthma, ye pussies.'

They know he's getting
too big for his boots
they all think it –
leaning against the fag wall.

The head crutcher,
(a right heel)
is losing face
he tells the asthma joker,

'You break
one of my crutches
I'll break
two of your legs'.

The leaners laugh last.

# Gretta's Hex

For years
Gretta cleaned
the factory
down the road from us.

When she had to have
her dog put down
because he had the mange

she got the runs
for three days.
Babbs Laffey
told the whole street.

Before this
she never missed work
not when her four girls
had the measles,
nor when the Pope came
to Ballybrit.

Now she went to the boss
she asked him for time off
to mourn her dead dog
she had long before the four girls
who recovered well from measles.

The boss said,
'Sorry Ann
I mean Gretta
1 can't spare you now
what with Sadie,
I mean Annie, on holiday
and the two Marys out sick,

you're the only one here
who can operate that buffer.

Can't you mourn your dead dog here,
take an extra fifteen minutes
at tea break, good girl.'

All these foul noises
from the boss's mouth
upset Gretta
who never missed
a cleaning factory
four girls with measles
young people of Ireland
Pope filled Ballybrit day
in her life.

From her grief stricken
dead dog hole in the heart
she wished him:

Sightreducingweekendsahead
buffer festering
the company of bats
the company of bees (over-tired and hungry ones)
nouns with genitive singular inflection

verbs with janitor holding injections
slow dipping in the wallet (by others)
Sadie and the two Marys
and above all
sleepus interruptus with demonos oftenus
plus an extra fifteen minutes in hell.
Amen.

# Prism

After the man
up our street
stuck broken glass
on top of his back wall
to keep out
those youngsters
who never stopped
teasing his
Doberman Pinscher,

he put
the safety chain
on the door,
sat at the kitchen window,
let out a nervous laugh
and watched
the Castle Park sun
divide the light
and scatter it
all over his property.

# The Temptation of Phillida

When she was younger
much younger
she liked to look deep
into men's eyes.
A friend told her
men can make you come
with their eyes.

One day at the traffic lights
she saw eyes
she wanted to fall into.

The owner of these baby blues
was leaning against the jewellery shop window
sucking a woodbine.
She kept looking deeper and deeper
she could see sapphires, rubies, white gold.
Eternity rings, paternity rings
gold rings gold things
every conceivable carat
heart in hand rings
heart in bag rings
heart in honey rings
O honey.

'Do you fuck?' said the woodbine.

'Only men with big crocodiles,' she said.

He threw the butt down and walked away.

She called after him,

'Is your crocodile
finger licking good
or index finger big?'

He started to run.

## Spiked

On the way to court
they did the caterpillar crawl,
all hitting the same stride
jumpers hanging
long beyond the fingers.

They quarter-filled the court
'Grievous Bodily Harm'
was up again
this time it wasn't too bad
only assault with menaces
and a wheel brace.

The caterpillar crew hooted
when he back-cheeked the judge,
the judge warned
and warned again.

When the court adjourned for lunch
they sat in the long hall
on the back of seats
walkmans, talkmans,
gum gobblers.

Maria who and Kelly what,
Jimmy and Sonia
always a Sonia
praising their idol to the skies,

the leather jacket cut of him
how he sorted that judge
how he turned round
and gave the fist
bare faced
fearing nothing and no one.

More smoke
rings were made
butts were flicked in the air
a thousand curses
court was back in session.
'Grievous' made more jestures
finger and fist
and fist again.

The pillar crew were roused
they whistled
through their fingers
in unison
no calming them now,

'cept when the judge
passed sentence
giving 'Grievous'
four of the best
to be served on Spike.

Lower lips
were dropping
eyes were welling
mascara was getting smeared.
A girl with a spiral perm
addressed the court,

'I'll write
every day Grevie,
promise you will too.'

'Sure babe, why wouldn't I?'

He made a fist
with the free hand
he boxed the air
they cheered
he made a fist again,

soon the free hand
was cuffed
no more fist in the air
he gave them the chin.

They knew what he meant.

# Night Noon and Nora

He was dead
no two ways about it
only his bones
never hit the clay
they were home
hitting the roof
when visitors came
he didn't want company
he only wanted her
not to leave him
to his thoughts
and his tea-stained eyes.

Master of mime,
he put on fantasy stockings
he sat on fantasy chairs
he called her
night noon and Nora,
the woman he nearly married
forty years ago
the woman whose husband Pious
got back cancer
from carrying her troubles.

He went for a spoon
and he brought back a fish.
Once at Eyre Square, he cried,
'I don't know who I am
promise you'll never leave me Nora
even when I'm asleep.'

Her word was gospel,
she got tired nodding
but she never slept,
except for the forty winks last September.
She remembered every wink
like thick soup, she said.

She went to grief counsellors,
she told them
bones in the house
spirit in the sky
stockings that aren't there

chairs that are no chairs
fish that are spoons
he's calling me Nora
I'm Bridget on the brink of a breakdown
help me.

They told her to let go
and let ever loving God
do night watchman.

The last straw was when
he turned up at second Mass
wearing only a lost look,
his clothes were at home
on the back of a chair,
a real chair.

She screamed out
to her ever loving God,
'I'm Bridget on the brink of a breakdown,
deliver me.'

God wasn't in at the time
he was down in Middle street
making mince meat out of Pious's cancer,
everyone knew that.

FROM AN AWFUL RACKET
(2001)

# Bare Bones

                        NATHANIEL LEE


The house is topsy-turvy
with the painters
when they knuckle down
me and Lickspittle dislocate
(he's the cat)
his joints are in the hall
skull 'n' doss-bone
one or two on the stairs
(he's devil jointed)

Mine too are hither and thither
a few on the landing not moving
only good for tripping over and over
I tell a lie one dropped down and down
a heavy hoor nearly killing the meter man
who to give him his due never howled
he only went click, click, click.

Lickspittle's joints are here
miscellaneous splashes are there
I'm running scissor rings around the room
losing weight as I rotate.

If they move one more of my things
I'll make no bones about it
I'll tell the painters
(one of whom is my husband)

If you move one more of my things
you'll meet treble fibula with a scissor complex
and you'll go down and down
as true as mother is in her grave.

And you may not have
the meter man to break your fall
or give you his fountain due
and the only sound you'll hear
will be clack, clack, clack, everywhere.

# The River

The shyness was painful,
before this not even the whisper
of a stolen kiss.

On the walk down towards the bridge
her head fitted his shoulder –
Gráinne's bed.

Wistful river
pulsating with greed
taking bits of everything
empty cigarette packets
(a lipstick wearer's handbag)
pieces of wood
her inhibitions.

Brazen sorcerer
never taking no for an answer,
all this slushing and gushing.

In no-time shyness slipped off her hips;
tonight she would wear lipstick
she would be young girl giddy
she would pirouette for nothing

she would show him her arse.

# Soft as Putty

The judge stopped him going down
for clocking the bouncer
with a sock full of snooker ball.

His mother pleaded gentle jelly
wouldn't kill a fly boy
soft as putty, my Mickey.

Framed, she cried, framed,
'cos he looked grown up
with the lone eyebrow,
the sheared ear,
the ring in the lip,
the bottom lip,
wouldn't kill a maggot,
Mickey, my Mickey.

She told your honour, my honour
about how long her Mickey
would keep fifty wasps alive in a jar
before rolling them out
for the cat to curl
with his claw,
the claw of his left paw.

He could do community service –
he could work in an aviary,
he has a way with birds,
the gait of our canary;
he could work in a beeviary,
he has a way with bees.

My honour was impressed –
he said, clear the court,
clear it now, pretty please.

## You'd Know He Had a Lovely Mother

He was in and out
of Madden's everyday,
always laughing.
He couldn't care less
about the weather,
or the tax on new shoes.

He spent hours
messing with the kids,
doing the three card trick,
blind man's bluff, ring-a-roses
or pin the tail.
He drove the dog up the walls
saying 'Where's the cat?'

He gave old Mrs Madden a hard time
about the artic licence she needed
for that wheelchair,
not to mention the brake fluid.
You're a right *scéiméir* was all she said,
as he spun her round the kitchen.

The bingo girls called him
'two little ducks'
on account of his arse
was so close to the ground.

He told them
if they weren't careful
he'd be the Clark Gable
to get into their knickers.
He'd give them clickety click all right.

They could shout check for a line across
but he was only scoring at the goal-post.
At this they howled,
blowing smoke in his face.

Then one day
before spring
he folded his clothes,
climbed the seventy-eight steps
to the tank near the reservoir
and flung himself in.

Three days later they found him
face down and dead.

After the funeral
Mrs Madden said,
you'd know he had a lovely mother
the way he folded them clothes.


## Pater

I was
dodging him
for years.

Now he's dead
I'm dying
for his shadow.


## Mother and Son
*(after Aleksander Sokurov)*

*I'd like to walk first,*
*let sleep be second;*
*let sleep always be second,*
*in fact let sleep be last.*

It's very cold now mother,
when you wake up it will be warmer.
We can walk then to the postcard bench,
I'll read the years back to you.
I'll ask 'who was he' questions,
you'll pretend not to hear me.
I won't ever mind mother.

I want to walk but I have no clothes,
only that raincoat that smells of death.
How can I walk in a raincoat
that smells of death?

Listen to her, no clothes indeed,
what next I ask you?
We can keep ourselves to ourselves,
just you and me mother.
We don't need raincoats or people,
we can stay away from people.

I'll wrap a blanket round you
and carry you most of the way.
You, light as the air,
I'll hardly know I'm carrying you.

I'll know my gentle son,
I'll always know you are carrying me,
my bones will be breaking with pity.


## For Crying Out Loud
*(a response to Leopardi's 'The Calm After the Storm')*


Listen Leo love,
pardon me for saying so
but that cockaleekie
about the storm
is hard to stomach.

A little less
of your lethargic lingo
would go a long way.

In other words Leo love
lighten up.

I'm no Prospero,
I'm the cabbage seller
and my study
is the streets.

A storm to you
is a drop in a bucket to me,
if I don't come out crying
I will end up eating cabbage,
my own cabbage
and nothing but cabbage

Nature is bounteous
when they buy my cabbage.
If I were to listen to you
you'd have me imagine
I sell my cabbage.

That's no good Leo love
*live horse and you'll get grass*
is up to snuff in airy fairy poems
but the cabbage seller must eat.
I have seven more
cabbage heads at home.

Anyway what storm were you on about?
I was there remember,
I felt no gust or gale,
storm in your head-cup was all.

If I feed them your theories
on what death heals us from,
on despair, on the misery of man,
they'd eat me alive
leaf by gangrenous leaf.

# Anthem

Our fury was well invested
year in, year out.
I wouldn't give an inch,
you wouldn't give an inch.
Hammer and tongs our anthem.

On the morning you died
I could see no reason
to change the habits of a lifetime.

It was strange
saying the rosary round your bed –
half praying, half miming.
The room was cold
with that window open.
Some *piseog* or other was being acted out.
(Letting your spirit dander round Mervue.)

A half-smoked cigarette
lay nipped on your bedside locker,
no *piseog* here only you were probably dying for a drag;
your new fur-lined slippers in everyone's way,
you weren't planning to leave just yet.

The rosary was in full flight –
echoes of the old days
and every bit as long
half song, half whisper,
extra prayers for the devil knows what.

As far as I was concerned
you had died, end of story
end of our Trojan War.

Some nuisance more ancient
than your Conamara lingo
or the jagged stones of Inis Meáin
was playing puck with my sensible side,
the side I use for dancing,

making me for the smallest whisker of a second
want to tuck the blankets round you,
sparing you the waspish November chill.

# Why I Refuse To Be Gracious

*the hee-goat spleen rosteth, helpeth the coeliack*
PLINY

My small intestine is anything but fine –
in fact my small intestine is anything but mine.
I have some of the most tangled and shrouded
reasons to whine, but do I ever, I never.

It's the gluten you see
and it hates the shite of me.
That jejunum the bugger
is the cause of all the trouble.
He does a handstand
when a chocolate bar he sees
or battered fish
or bread or cakes or custard creams.

When he's supposed to work
he'll throw a wobbler,
acts gimped or look inane
and carp and carp and malabsorb
until the stone of unripe grape
is portion plenty at the gate.

The inner circle talk now going round
is about the cleanest colon in town –
I'm pissed off it will never ever be me.

My mucosa makes the mosta
of my slighest little boasta
my villi is the dilli with the willi
in the middle of a field
each villus that should stand
just flops to beat the band
waiting myrtles and quinces
and shredded fifty pences.

My enterocytes acts the shitists
in the middle of the nightists
and the he-goat spleen
is nowhere to be seen
roasted or raw
or ready for the thaw
not a drop not a jigger
not a lick of the frigger
have I sampled since I was eighteen

# The Chamber Pit

Through the chair Mayor
at the last meeting
or the meet before the estimates
I did propose that we congratulate
the man who put up the lovely crib.

I know I got a seconder,
I always get a seconder,
my proposals are legendary
for getting seconders,
but c'mere Mayor
through the chair
the trouble is
my proposal isn't here.

I'm not saying nothing
and this isn't a whine
only when a man
who's had as much tragedy
as the crib man
goes round and puts up a crib of that calibre
the least we can do
is the least we can do.

Not in any cap in hand way,
cribbers hate that malarky,
cribbers hate oligarchy,
it should come from
the pit of the councillors' chambers
which is often a snake pit
as we all know, ha ha.

Rumours about his wife
being a right dog in the manger
for running off with the coal man
just after he changed to Polish coal
are neither here nor there.

The crib man never complained
about her indiscretions before this,
when there was talk she did it with a bishop,
when anyone with half a brain knows
bishops don't do it for Christ's sake.

This carry-on is rumour heavy
and cropped up long before
the coal man started selling bottled gas on the side
(she always said he was a gas man).

Leaving aside bishops and gas bottles
the point is through the chair Mayor
that her cribbie sculpted the realest looking
baby Jesus and three of the wisest looking men
with duffle coats and slingback sandals
who looked like they came straight out of Galway Bay
on a wet day long before the treatment plant
got the bum's rush.

I think we should be on the hands and knees
of this cribbie not to mind bothering
about the shadows in his wife's past.

Polish coal and Papal Nuncios
could never burn as bright
as the star he sculpted
out of that gone-off asbestos.

If we play our cards right this year
who knows next year
he might get the baby Jesus –
real looking as he is –
down off the lean-to roof
and land him in a bed of crisp dry straw.

## Our Mothers Die On Days Like This

When there isn't a puff
and the walk from the bus stop
to the front door
isn't worth the longed-for
out-of-the-question cup of sweet tea
she can never have
because doctor do-little-or-nothing
told her face to face
it was the sugar or the clay
the choice was hers.

The choice was no choice
he knew it, she knew it.

When the heavy bill on the hall floor
with the final notice reminded her
once and for all she must turn out the lights,
her Angelus bell rang and rang.

## The Weather Beaters

The bitter snap is over,
a few bones told them.
The two of them leg it
through the green
a hundred steps more or less
and the cure will be in hand.

The winter was too long,
this is the first bright day
and true to form
pep came back to step
it out across the Prairie,
the only open space in Castle Park.

They are not as old as they look,
these weather beaters,
karate-expert weather beaters,
they box it and kick it
with their falling off toes,
they shout while they do it,
one says the snow is an animal,
a pig-dog with warts the other says.

This bright day has given them hope,
antifreeze-cider-hope,
they're walking faster now,
they leg it across the green
faster than they did in ages.

The flea-infested couch they got
as a so-called Christmas present
can go to blazes,
they think this in unison
with their bachelor brains.

Today they stretch their bones,
their funny bones,
everything is funny today –
they say hello to two kids lighting a fire,
the kids say fuck off and die,
the weather beaters laugh and laugh.

## The Fracture

The man in number seven
is waiting for God to call him.
He has lived long enough,
he has lived too long.

The worst thing is lighting the fires,
first in the kitchen then the sitting-room
same old ding dong.
Some days there is no draught
and when there is no draught there is no flame.

This day out of the deep blue
his thoughts seemed to cosy up to one another
they held a playful pattern, he was glad of it,
he would take their lead.

He brought the telly into the kitchen –
only thing is the kitchen has no comfortable chair.
After a lengthy battle on the rights and wrongs of it
a lone thought emerged, it told him what to do.

He dragged the armchair
from the front room to the back room
nicking his hip in the process.
(luckily it was his span new hip
not the other one, a feather fall would fracture)
The kitchen was too small
the kitchen table would have to go.

When herself was here
lighting the fires was a work of art
the tightly twisted paper first
the kippings he collected on their daily walks
the cinders from yesterday
the small coals on top
rising to a pyramid of love.
In no time they would interpret the sparks.

This day his thoughts were in a hurry
he held the reins long enough
he held the reins too long
the pattern was ravelled
the feather did fall.

He didn't like lighting fires
he didn't like eating off his lap
he didn't like the way the sunlight
crept into his kitchen in the mornings
and reminded him of things.

His world was tearing, the big split –
a sheet caught in barbed wire.
The kitchen table was out the back
the front room was now the back room
the kitchen was becoming the bedroom
upstairs was now downstairs.

Another lone thought prodded –
outside is not inside,
outside will always stay outside
out there will never get you in here
not today, not tomorrow
not the week after the races
not two weeks before Saint John's night.

That's right the old man reckoned
with a gush of youth in his veins
there is no why
there is no where
there is only out there
and it will stay out there
until the flames of hell smoulder and die.

# Good Friday in Majorca

He said to her that morning,
this is going to be the day mama,
the day of all days.
No more Peach Schnapps in my porridge mama,
today Christ died for us,
today I will let people live,
and another thing mama –
this will be a free ride on my bus day.

He let everyone on his bus,
he let on their relations,
after that the people on the next street,
everyone on the next four streets;
he took no pesetas,
he spoke in sangria and sign
in, in, in, Schwein Hunde
and Wie Geht's your arse,
I love Jerusalem, get in, get in.

He let on all the grandfathers and grandmothers
and the great-grandmothers,
the place was crawling with great-grandmothers
and all the people he had met over the years
on his daily journey from Ar'enal to Palma.

He got all the grand people
and the great people to squash against the door,
some slid sideways to the ceiling,
the great-grandmothers were good at that,
he was pass remarkable about their knitting,
he said I hope you did not bring your knitting today
old mamas this is not a knitting day,
today we go to Palma to the procession.
He turned the air conditioning off,
he turned the loud music on –
soccer winning music,
Coppa Coblana stuff.

He didn't stop when the people pressed the bell,
red lights didn't matter or signs or arrows
or a million lemons,
in fact he gave the arrows the sign,
he gave the signs the finger, the middle finger,
he gave the lemons the bad eye –
'lemons lemons I see nothing but lemons'.

He told the people from Siesta Street to move back,
he abused them a bit, saying he had it from a good source
that they would sleep on knitting needles.
He warned them about harbouring chickens
under overcoats on Good Friday;
he said, them days are gone
this is Good Friday
not suckling pig Sunday –
we are going to market,
we are going to Palma to the procession,
enjoy the music.

After a while people thought
there might be an announcement –
the people were right,
once the rose window of La Seu Cathedral
came into view the bus driver said,

Amigos, today is Good Friday this is my bus –
you are getting a free ride all the way to Palma,
sit back on your neighbour,
get close to the one from the next street,
never you mind the crowd from Siesta Street,
they are all dreaming of roast suckling pig.
I have watched you over the years –
you are too standoffish,
squash in there; be in touch with your neighbour.
Christ died for you, you die a little today,
today is Good Friday, this is my bus
we go all the way to Palma.

A few grandfathers started to scream.
I knew it, I knew it, said the driver
I knew the grandfathers would be first to scream.
Shame on you old man
just because you are in your eighties
and people are sitting on your head –
look at that poor mama in the corner turning blue
do you hear her screaming?

I know you have a chicken inside that coat
because nobody could have a belly that size.

I knew the moment I saw you
you were the chicken hiding type,
you get a free ride all the way to Palma

and what do you do, you scream and whine,
you have two chickens inside your coat
I'm sure of it, you have it written all over your face.

Some brave grandmother plucked up the courage
to shout at the driver,
not the one going blue but a second cousin of hers
from Santa Ponsa up for the weekend.
Loco, she said, Loco.

The driver didn't like it,
he always said he hated back cheek from grandmothers
who had turning blue cousins up from Magalluf or Santa Ponsa.
Screams from chicken shitters would be one thing
but this was too much for him

Mama he said, this is Good Friday, this is my bus –
it may have a few dints from the narrow corners,
there may be a ladder swinging from the roof
where the painter tried to sneak on without paying,
if he had tried the front door like everyone else
he would know it was a no peseta day,
out of the goodness of my big heart
I bring you and half the neighbourhood
and their squakie kids
and grandfathers who think
I don't know the smell of chicken shit,
I bring you all to Palma
for the procession non-stop all the way
for no pesetas,
en route you see a million lemons
you bitter bastards,
I give you Copa Coblana loud as you like
and you call me loco
you said it twice
loco, you said, loco
mama are you crazy
get off my bus.

# The Clemson Experience

*(Conference of Irish Studies. Conference centre*
*surrounded by golf course, formerly a plantation)*

In the Walker Golf Course where no one walked
Joyce's wet dreams were splashed about
in the name of the father.
Carson's bullets slip-jigged and reeled,
Yeats's black habits were boiled and peeled
more Joyce dot.com for psycho-netters –
Joyce in Celluloid, Joyce in hotpants,
Joyce in toilet with betters.

Heaney's bogmen were dragged up
by their rotting stubs,
their bones picked asunder,
the contents of their ancient bellies
made flesh and flung amongst us
on this golf course at Clemson, once a plantation
where tailgating is something dirty Yeats didn't do.

The golfers over-the-hilled it at 8 a.m.
in their twenties, in their trolleys, off their trolleys
on their starter's orders.

The man with the megaphone threw shapes.
'Proper golf attire does not include
grown men with big bellies prancing round
this 18 hole in suspender belts,
shorts should be of Bermuda persuasion
not to the shins or below
not too far above the knees,
no balls in the trees,
that last remark was a slip of the tongue.

Right you cock shots, you hot shots,
only collared shirts here,
shiftless losers over there,
no flashy ankle socks with tiger paws or other,
absolutely no swimwear, no Aran sweaters –
if you want Synge try Ballroom Four.'

Papers about what Jack B did to Lady G
while W.B. was exorcising his tea
or viewing *A Portrait* from his tightest orifice (with slides)
chaired by a Carolina Panther supporter from Chattanooga

154

or the pitying shape of Irish drama
as told through the space invaders in Friel's work
or learning the quotable Yeats and Heaney in three easy lessons
for after dinner speeches or the odd peace process.

Megaphoner-all-aloner was losing it with the golfers.

'Hey you, Mr Inappropriate chest of drawers
do you want me to send you in there
where they pick Heaney, poke Joyce,
pickle the bones from man of ice,
O.D. on Yeats and queer theory,
Tiresias and Art O'Leary.

Where all day is spent finding the missing link
between Behan, Boland and Lewinsky.
And you with the black leggings,
put your hand on your affliction
when I am dressing you down.

This is Clemson, home of The Clemson Tigers
where the Blue Ridge Mountains shield you
from the smell of that rotting cheese,
where Lake Heartwell ducks eat gluten-free bread,
where the azaleas and camellias
would sicken a sorry dog with that splash of colour,
where the chrysanthemums are edging in just for notice.

The choice is yours, will you wear proper golfing attire
or will I let the wind-filled professors at you?
Where they heaney time by plucking the maggots
and sucking the marrow out of the bones of the bogmen of Ireland
on this championship golf course, once a plantation.
What's it to be, you in the girl's knickers!'

# They Always Get Curried Chips

Between her supermarket singsong
and the endless gossip she loves
Dolly's voice is nearly gone.

What scandal the builders throw her
is piffle, compared to when
the sisters-in-law come round.

Every extension is taken apart
brick by adulterous brick,
they know the footfall
and back-to-front baseball cap

of every builder who's doing it
with the wife's sister
or that skinny wan with the hippy hair,
they know him down to the birthmark
on his lovely arse.

They see the cracks in every
brick and mortar give-and-take
that was hammered out in back seats
below in condom alley valley,

where the hoods sell Ecstasy
and good for nothing cars
with nare a number plate
never mind a log book.

The extension is the thing –
they call it the granny flat,
it takes the harm out of it
like, one owner, mint condition
woman driver kind of shite.

It's not just small talk, it's all talk –
instead of good morning
it's good extension,
happy May day has become
happy granny flat day.

'She has three and a half kids and a lean-to'
(god bless the mark),
'my rafter's going up a Friday',

'my plumber is nearly upon me',
'my roofer is roofing like billy-o'.

Where will the big dogs go now
that's what I'd like to know
at the end of our row
there's one as big as a horse.

They keep him
and his four sets of teeth
in a back yard
full of broken busses and road signs,
the new extension will cover him,
an overcoat of concrete,
molar drive.

Dolly's new extension
will take your eye out,
it will have every doodad.
A couch that won't burn
no matter what
buttons that bring on the footstools,

a picture of a boy in blue
with a tear on his cheek,
a remote control
that dominates the curtains,
a dining-room table
that goes inside itself,
a grandfather clock that belts out rave
and Spanish sign language.

The extension means more than space,
her status will rise in the estate
so it was written on the bingo book.

The extension will tower above the hedge
the neighbours fashioned
to stop seeing Dolly
smoke a chunk of midweek.

As for the two-up and two-downers
she pities them, she'd tell you herself.
I pity them poor bastards
with nothing to show for themselves
only two-ups and two-downs.

Look at me, I could keep lodgers,
I could keep a small village in that granny flat
and still have room to spare
when the sisters-in-law come round.

And come round they do and often
they talk back-to-front-baseball caps
they talk shape, they talk size
when it comes to it
size is everything,
they talk backseat gobbledegook,
nothing is really sacred,

mind you they don't do politics or piss artists
but they do do priests, and how.
Tired of talking, it's time for food,

they always get curried chips,
they rarely get planning permission.

## Snakes and Ladders

Deckie is out polishing the car again –
they think they got a great deal,
a great steal would be more like,
it's all paint and powder.

It was wrapped round a pole the other week,
the headlights doing buck and swing,
the chassis doing mime –
it's stitched together,
a goat in silk knickers.

Speedin down Claw Hammer Drive –
gadgets, geegaws, speakers,
Man United stickers,
furry things hanging from the dash,
the engine left sitting at the traffic lights.

Annie will bate seven shades out of him
give her anything but engines left sitting at traffic lights –
she wears the trousers in that house,
she wears the house in that trousers,
no sansculotte about that biddy,
she's trousered to the gills.

Deckie was shifted once
after she caught him shaggin' Picasso
she told him to wise up
and get the diesel out of his eyes.

The shagger still moults around
but the shaggin' is supposed to be done with
according to a local swing bag who doubles up
as a window leaner with a flair for
cock-cooling and garden gnome counselling.

But some of us plebs know better
when Deckie is off work and Annie is in town
old Picasso acts the sidewinder
armed with his paintbrush
his bulging trousers,

he keeps his ladder in his underpants.

## The Lads Said He Was a Sissy

He walks
up and down the green
with a bag full of stones
and his tiny dog –
the dog is always knackered,
you never saw such a pissed-off dog.

All day everyday,
walk walk bag of stones,
tired dog.

Some say he carries china
from the china factory
where he worked,
but it doesn't clink
and the struggle is too great,
it must be stones.

Years ago
he was a flasher,
he lived opposite our school.
At lunch time he would stand naked
in the window
and play with his genitals.

We're going to see the flasher,
'any takers' was the catch cry –
we went, we saw,
none of us said much
only, what's on him?
The lads said he was a sissy.

It broke the monotony
of who made the world
and why did she make the world?

He calls the dog Tartarus,
other times he called him
piss-head or come on wagon.

When Television came to Ballybrit
we were ready for it.

# April Fool's Day in Jerusalem

The soldiers were everywhere –
running up and down steps,
in and out of this street,
this way that way zigzag way
around corners in their twenties.

I asked what was going on.
It's nothing, the man said,
they have to circumnavigate
and go through the streets,
and go through the houses,
they zigzag a little,
they up and down a little,
they around corners a lot,
it's nothing, enjoy the sunshine.

# The Bag Boat

All's ya done was
went down in the morning,
put your back against the wall
and hoped that the stevedore
would give you the beck.

If he did
you navvied like the Firbolg
until the slings were full.

If forty bags a sling
was all they took,
you wouldn't give a damn
but you knew
you were giving more or less
than you would ever get back.

If one drop of rain fell
not one fertiliser bag
did you swing.

There was nothing for it
but jack up and go the pub.
One drop was an act of God,
two drops was a hurricane.

If you didn't get picked
you went home
taking misery with you,
of that you had a sackfull.

The ones with the docker's card
had it sewn up,
they were always picked,
hand picked, the cunts.

## She Believed in Miracles

He was a painter
a house painter
he loved white
he wore white overalls
all the week,
overall he wore white
nice and tight
around the bum,
his car was white
his wife was white
she wore white ski pants
and a white tank top
she loved the tank top,
she loved the big top as well
but not as much as the tank top.

He told anyone who listened
that his mother was a falling down drunk,
he even told the priest Father Quirke.
Father father my mother
drinks herself under the table
every night, the white table.

Father Quirke didn't believe him
he knew that snowball's mother
was never in a pub in her life
the chemist shop now and again and again,
but never the pub
and if people don't see it
it doesn't happen.

At weekends Snowball liked to dress up –
his nice white slacks, a tasty white polo neck,
white gym shoes and crisp white sin free socks,
a key-ring with a white rabbit dangling from it,
he never went anywhere without the key ring.

He told welfare
his mother had a drink problem,
he begged them for carer's assistance;
I'm a carer, he says, assist me
but they didn't believe him.

He didn't get much for painting houses,
he would only paint white –
if you wanted any other colour,
he said, sorry mam no can do,
he always said no can do.

His mother never went to the pub
in fact she didn't much like other people
unless they were wearing white
then she would say, loveen I like your tank top.
In fairness to her, she did like rabbits.

When she died
they found eight hundred
and forty-five empty cough bottles
in the coal bunker.

Snowball was grand first
then the bad dreams came
every snake-headed whipper snapper turned up.
The furies had a regular bus pass,
the minute his eyes closed they pounced
licking the soles of his feet
with their wirebrush tongues.

They told him to make a sculpture
out of the cough bottles for all to see
otherwise two of his flat feet
would never again do a soft shoe routine
while he pulled a rabbit out of a can of paint.

Give him anything but naked fear
he says, give me anything but naked fear.
He set the sculpture in the front garden,
it took the shape of a hippogriff
perched in a monkey puzzle tree.

People tried not to look at it
but it was there and it was big,
eight hundred and something cough bottles big.

They say it had a cure for bad chests
all you had to do was look at it
and you were phlegm free forever.
Wheezers were coming from all over Ireland,
a few from the outer Hebrides,
a bus load from Inverness,

there was talk of a crowd
of long term dope-smokers
up from Bengal Bay;
they were the real huffers and puffers,
more talk about eighteen Bedouins
from the Judaean desert
who tried the Dead Sea
but still they coughed.

People came and people looked –
one fat fella with a foul mouth
and a really chalky wheeze
said he was in for the long haul,
said he wouldn't go home till a miracle happened.
He got pneumonia and died.
His wife told the local paper she believed in miracles.


## Lucky Mrs Higgins

When our mother
won a fridge
with Becker's Tea,
she got her photograph
in the *Sentinel*
shaking hands
with the man from head office.

The fridge was also
in the frame.
She wore a big wide hat
she kept on top of the wardrobe
for fridge winning days.

It went nice
with the crimplene two piece
she got for Mary Theresa's wedding.

In the photo
with the fridge
and the man from head office
she didn't look anything like herself.

# Our Brother the Pope

*Sorrow is better than laughter,*
*for by a sad countenance the heart is made better.*
ECCLESIASTES


Few people know this
but Pope John the 23rd
was a member of our family.
His real name was
Pope John the 23rd Higgins.

He lived with us in Ballybrit,
I can't say he had his own room
but he didn't need it;
he had his own house,
our house.

He was there
when our father
brought home the mackerel,
when Yahweh Curran
whistled his way
round the twelve cottages.

He was there when we
painted the house
for the races
and when we
got the new range
Stanley the 9th.

When he died
nothing was the same.
The mackerel began to stink,
Yahweh Curran didn't whistle
for a solid month,
the picture show in Silk's Shed
was just a runaway wagon
with three wheels.

Our mother cried and cried.
Saint Jude and Saint Agnes
let her down big time,
as for poor Philomena,
she couldn't conjure up

a minor miracle if her life depended on it,
she was gone by the board.

The neighbours who were well clued in
queued up round the cottages
to offer their condolence,
they were soaking in grief.

We're sorry about the mackerel
they said one after the other,
holding their noses.
Our mother cried louder.

# Hey Greggie

I didn't mind
sleeping in the shed,
it wasn't every night
for crying out loud,
only the nights
he had a skinful – bang.

I knew as true
as there's shit in a duck
that one day he'd get his –
and he did – quack.

He fell
and hit his head
off the garden wall – smack.

When he went down
he stayed down
big and all as he was – boing!

I'm still collecting his pension
and he's three years dead now.
I have lunch out
in the Imperial every week
and it's on him – clack.

The fall made a hole in his head,
a clean hole all things considered,
you'd fit a farmer's hand inside it – whack.

Every week in the Imperial
I drink to him –
I say, hey Greggie!
may you rot in hell-swell.


## City Slicker


When Killer Kelly
drove past at speed
*Mott the Hoople* blazing,
with one hand out the window
holding the roof like a trophy
and Baby Keogh caught a glimpse
from the safer side of lace,
she thought for one split second
she could crush his lovely head with her thighs
and never throw any backwater priest the details
she knew the city had snaked into her veins.

# My Face Goes Scarlet

*The only time kids these days went on their knees
is when they are giving blow jobs*

FR. JOHN KERRANE
Dunshaughlin, Co. Meath,
Irish Times, 4 December 1999


I'm sick of it
I've had it up to there.
They never stop
every night
its the same thing,
week in
week out.

They start hanging around the wall
in sixes and sevens,
if they're not smoking dope
they're sniffing glue.

And if they're not
sniffing glue
they're up the backs
giving blow-jobs.

And I wouldn't mind
some of them
wouldn't blow snow
off a rope.

My face goes scarlet
when I see them youngsters
on their knees.

I shout at them
I say, go on outa that, ye pups
but they're far too employed.

You know who I blame,
I blame the parents
for not wearing protection.

# He Knows About Cars

The man with the greyhounds
knows about cars
though he never drove himself.
When he walks the dogs
he writes crime novels in his head.
When he hits a full stop you know it.
It's the chin, eyes and upper torso swing
that give him away.
The comma is more of a wobble than a fall.

On one leash he has six greyhounds,
on the other he has a light-hearted mongrel
whose feet hardly touch the ground.

She's a big jellyfish that one,
I have to bring her everywhere.
They'd eat her alive if I left her with them.
See that dint in her back,
they thought she was a hare once
and there was a quare hullabaloo,
skin and hair flying was nothing.

She's a great little watchdog though,
she hates the postman,
he knows too much for his small head –
he starts off about soccer
and he ends up
talking about stocks and shares
and Legionnaire's Disease,
on top of him being master mind
he's a scandal monger.

My neighbour was under the car one day
looking for his child's tooth
(the tooth fairy was a joy-rider).
The unwelcome soothsayer
with letters after his name
got down on his knees
and gawked in at him
that's how nosy we're talking.

The thing about cars is
when it's frosty
you should never
leave the wipers fifty fifty
'cos next morning
when you're turning her on
they'll snap
like a postman's knee.


## The Sentence


Chatterina plucked pregnant pauses
out of the lips of good neighbours
and knitted them into
a thousand words per minute.

Himself measured words,
his phrases had short back and sides,
his verbs were anorexic
his nouns were Hail Holy Queens,
he mouthed the tight-rope of caution,
he was fond of the silent 'e'.

Chatterina was tell a tale and tell it well
and wrap it round a light-pole
and weave it up and down this estate
type of person. On top of that she was clean.

One day she was telling us about how
the Corporation tried to evict her
because she wasn't wearing the orange lipstick
set out in article two of the leasing agreement.

She was galloping to the finish line
with words jam packed with pig-eyed plurals and steam
when a frog got caught in her throat.

After the stroke
himself finished her sentence.

## They Never Wear Coats

They start early on Friday night
in the girlfriend's house.
They pour into the new clothes
from Fenwicks
or the bargain rail.

These tubes on legs,
high heels on stilts,
will paint the town red.
A swig for you,
a swig for me –
'that looks lovely on ya hinny,
I'd nearly do ya meself.'

With perfect Revlon faces
they hit Newcastle
linking each other
six or seven across.
Close enough to trade
secret for Geordie secret.

When eleven comes
they fall from grace
onto the night club queue.
Carol as always has to pee,
'Have ya had a good look like,
I'll shove yer face in it for ya?'

More laughter, eye contact is made
the bonding started long before this
in another pub in the Bigg Market.
A glance that lingers longer than a second
is at least the promise of a blow job.

They look like models,
same shakey walk,
same knicker jaw-line,
they never wear coats.

The bouncers can look all they like
through their gable-end shoulders.
They have close shaves,
they have no necks,
they list on the soles of their feet,

a practised technique.
They say one of them done it for a week
without blinking.
The money raised went to
the battered bouncers ball.

In the lane
near Tyneside Cinema
earlier glances are being metamorphosed.
Shadows fumble, they nearly fall
with heart-stopping ticks of lust.

They know the words of all the songs,
they sing them all day in the workplace.
*'I try to say goodbye and I choke.*
*I try to walk away and I stumble.'*
This night they sing louder
helped by vodka and gin.

Again they link their precious friends,
they are ready for Geordie,
no need to beat around the bush,
they speak his language.

'I'll shag him the neet
and he won't know what hit him,
big Geordie fuck.'

## The Visionary

The woman in the sweet shop
is turning into her mother.
Only the other week
she was young
when talk of weddings,
wallpaper, new fridges
and a small flat in the town was all talk.

Then for God knows why
he took a bus that never stopped
and she was left
with the wallpaper shame
of not having any fruit in her womb
that she might buy
white socks for.

Her mother's tiredness
grew into her,
her mannerisms,
her thanks be to Gods.

When she totted up the numbers
she wore her mother's glasses.
She joked about it,

'Sure what difference does it make
haven't me and mammy
the same vision anyway,
aren't we both far-sighted?'

# An Awful Racket

In the winter
we don't light a fire everyday,
three days a week max
always on a Saturday night though.

Me and the kids sit around the fire
and sing songs, the twins clap,
they play Baker's Man
we have great craic,
except for Justin
I nearly had him in a taxi
that's why we called him Justin.

He's fourteen now, he's always angry.
'What good is looking into the fire like spas,
what's fuckin wrong with ye?' he says.

Then all hell breaks loose.
I don't allow fowl language,
I didn't bring them up like that,
then the twins start bawling
and I can't shut them up.
The eldest starts first,
he was born ten seconds before Paul.
I say to Peter, 'If you don't shut that
fucking cake hole, I'll throttle ya.'
Then Paul starts,
he has lungs like a broken exhaust.

Last year when things
were a bit slack
we burned their father's wardrobe.
We split up two years ago,
we parted on amiable grounds though.
I couldn't aim
And he couldn't miss.

The kids thought it was a howl
me taking a hatchet to the wardrobe
on Christmas Day.

There was nothing much in it anyway,
only a couple of his shirts
I'd forgotten to put in the mincer,
old papers where the cat had kittens
and a banjaxed tennis racket.

That racket caused more trouble;
one day no one wanted it,
the next day they all wanted it.
I ended up throwing it on the fire.

It crackled like lard.


## Succubus and Her Sisters


I haven't a hope in hell against Succubus
who comes to you in deep slumber
with her dying-for-it phantom sisters,
their bala-kelpie cleavage,
their coal-bucket eyes,
they dance around your bed
letting on to be rancour free, bereft of bile.

Just when you thought it was safe
to take a loving astral leap in my direction
another gang of shadowy nebulas
beckon to the goblins in malevolent hot-pants
who lurk on your landing
waiting to slither under your duvet
to hammer out ghoulish acts
unheard of in any ancient Sanskrit,

they leave you drained,
they don't leave you dry.

# Black Dog in My Docs Day

Your mother rings from your grave.
I say where are you?
She says, I'm at Michael's grave
and it looks lovely today.

Duffy misses you,
Jennifer Lydon misses you.
You were grand until depression
slipped into your shoes –
after that you dragged your feet
big long giraffe strides. Slim-2 Speed.

When depression slept
you were up for anything,
go for it and you went for it –
times you got it, other times you lost it,
you didn't play the lyre,
you played the horses,
lady luck was often with you
you never looked back
William and Lara miss you.

When you were a few months old
I went to see you in hospital,
you had meningitis.
The nurse told me that I had to leave,
I told her you were my nephew,
she said you still had meningitis.
You had days months and years to go,
the crowd in Maxwell's miss you.

When your mother said,
Michael started school today
I thought you were too young,
you grew up without telling us,
you went to sleep small,
when you got up
you were kitchen-table tall,
you had fourteen years to go.

A messer in your Communion photos,
leaning against the wall in hidden valley
arms akimbo, one foot behind the other,
you were ready to trip the light fantastic
the body of Christ.

Odd times in Castle Park
when you were passing the house,
I'd said, Michael wait up
you'd say, no way José!
I've got the black dog in my shoes
I have to drag him half way across Ireland ,
I have to do it today and it must be raining.

Our Jennifer misses you
Christy misses the long chats with you,
he wished you didn't talk so much in the bookies,
Heather misses you,
Larry didn't know you
but Larry misses you because Heather misses you.

Eleven years to go you dyed your hair,
your uncles didn't know you,
they didn't know what they were missing.
No school wanted you.
You wanted Nirvana, you wanted The Doors,
you wanted shoes you didn't have to drag
you wanted hush puppies or Gandhi's flip-flops
instead you got Docs with a difference
the joy-roy gang miss you.

For your Confirmation
you took Hercules as your middle name,
you wanted a sweatshirt and baggy pants,
you left your mother and George at the church,
kiss me there you said to your mother
pointing to your cheek
and you were off with your friends,
soldier of Christ.
Auntie Mary and Aidan miss you,
Johnny misses you,
Caroline Keady misses you.

Móinín na gCiseach Tech said you failed maths,
you went in yourself to set the record straight.
Your mother has the letter of apology the school sent.
No school wanted the boy with blue hair
Dana C. and Caroline L. miss you.

You did the junior cert
with 'Dóchas an Oige',
we went down on open day,
you made us cranky buns,

real conversation stoppers.
Bobby and Shane miss you.

The day you and I filled in
your passport application
your shoes were empty
except for your long dreamy feet,
they matched your fanciful answers.
Name: Michael drop-dead-gorgeous Mullins.
Who do you want to be when you grow up?
A rolling fucking stone baby
Keith The Buckfast Kid misses you,
Margaret and John miss you.

The black dog came and went,
he didn't answer to Lassie
but when you said, hey Cerberus!
an idiotic grin came over his dogface.
The tea-leaf who just got out misses you.

When I visited you in the Psych first
you were outside sitting next to
a bucketful of cigarette ends.
I said you'd need to cut down
on the fags or you'd end up killing yourself.
We laughed till we nearly cried.
Granny Bernie misses you
Alice and Brendan miss you
you had a year left give or take.

You talked a lot about your daughter Erin,
she was eighteen months you were eighteen years.
You were here she was over there.
You called to Father Frankie
and asked if one day you could have Erin baptised,
you were soaking to the skin that day,
you were always walking in the rain,
docs filled with despair day,
black dog in my docs day.
Jackie from the psych misses you.

The day you got out for the last time
you and I walked from our house to Carnmore.
We had a drink at the crossroads
You weren't supposed to with the medication.
Fuck it you said if all those smarties I took
didn't kill me a pint of pissie beer hardly will.

You showed me round the house,
you said it was spooky
and if you were going to top yourself
it would be here you'd do it, and you did.
Auntie Carmel in Florida misses you,
Jennifer said you had a girlfriend,
Linda misses you,
Claire from Waterside House misses you.

You wanted to fathom the world
but your legs were tired,
you had two months left.
Cookie and Jillian miss you.
You talked about the dark hole
you often found yourself in,
you were happy when you got out
but when you were in it,
there was no talking to you,
you had weeks to go.
The Rinnmore gang miss you.

You got a bad 'flu
and the 'flu got you
the Millennium Bug,
your days were numbered.

Depression and the 'flu didn't travel
but you did and you never came back.
On December the 9th 1999
you hanged yourself.
Paddy L. and Michael Flaherty miss you.

Your mother rings from your grave
I say where are you?
She says, I'm at Michael's grave
and it looks lovely today.

# They Never Clapped

*(after Sirkka-Liisa Konttinen)*


## *Valerie*

She was two the first time she came,
she cried and cried.
I told her mother
you're wasting my time and your money,
she's a crier not a dancer.
She dances at home the mother said.
Well let her stay at home I said,
I took no guff off them
at two or twenty.


## *Lily*

She did 'Sugar Plum Fairy'.
She got ninety seven out of a hundred,
ashen little pus on her.
She was bawling in her sleep,
she had the runs all morning,
but ninety-seven out of a hundred
not bad for three-and-a-half.


## *Dolly*

When I see her dancing there
I see me dancing there;
when people admire her
they admire me.
We live through our daughters,
everyone knows that.
After seven kids
I'm coming back to it,
I'll look the spit out of her
only older.
When the mothers go for bronze
I'll get it I know I will.
It's just my outlook on things.

## Dolores

She gets all her notions
from the telly that one,
she'd make a smashing child model
so finicky about her appearance
when she wears a dress for a couple of hours
she throws it in the wash basket,
this goes on all day every day.
On top of all that she'll only wear pink.
When I look in the laundry cupboard
and the washing is piled ten foot high
and it takes me four hours to iron it
I know I've trained her well.


## Carol

One of them is getting married on me,
she's pregnant by a married man
after all the money I spent on dancing lessons.
She is not marrying him thank God,
he's not worth it she says.
She wants to take my three-piece suite,
mind you she's only going round the corner.
I suppose I could sit on it in her house.
It wouldn't be the same though, would it?


## Sally

She could dance before she could walk,
we'd tie her to the back of the door on a pair of reins
and let her find her feet, she loved it.
Only problem was when you were having
a cup of tea you'd have to watch it,
nine times out of ten a leg would swing up,
my big hope was that one day
the two legs would work together
and she would make us proud
me and her father.

## Sonya

My lass had a chance
to do a part in Les Mis,
in London if you don't mind.
My neighbour says London how are ya?
She had an ear infection
the day of the audition.
I don't know about London
she dances on my tips here.
I'd have to be making awful big tips
if she was dancing in London.
After me and her father split up
the tips was everything
I told her straight to her face,
I said, Sonya love
my tips is all we've got.


## Florrie

The girls are measured every year,
if they don't grow at the right rate
they are out on their ear.
I always whisper to my lassie
when I'm tucking her in
mirror mirror on the wall
mirror mirror make her tall.
It's not their fault if they don't grow
and you tell them that,
you say it's not your fault if you don't grow,
at the same time you watch them
out of the corner of your eye.


## Rosie

The careers officer
called her an 'Outdoor girl',
she liked it, it sounded kind of dirty.
He said he'd bet she could dance
up the butter queue and not be out of breath.
She asked him in her best dancing accent
how long was the butter queue,
he told her straight up
three quarters of a man-made mile.

## Kelly

Her grandfather
sews all her dancing costumes
he's seventy, she's the apple of his eye.
All she does is wrap her legs
the wrong way round a chair,
drop her head forward,
peep out from behind her hair
in a certain way,
show him how she can lick her bottom lip
over and over
and he sews like billy-o.


## Annie

Eventually she had to get a right job
with her brains and all.
She was fifth in charge
in a psychiatric ward.
Late at night in her leotards
(which were done to death in rhinestones)
she practised for the patients,
she did them ballroom and tap the odd tango,
they never clapped.

# The Jugglers

## 1 *The Jugglers*

The Corpo bunged us all together
as part of some high and mighty pilot project,
it's high and mighty all right
but the lifts don't work.

The gangs know we are all lone parents,
they give you a cold stare
scares me to death but I never let on,
you have to act tough,
you have to grow a second skin;
mine's a tiger skin,
I wear it everywhere,
when I pass the druggies on the stairs
I growl, I make like I'm vicious,
I have to otherwise you're fair game.

The guys storing stolen property are just as bad,
they whizz by you at break-neck speed,
they'd knock you down as quick as they'd look at you;
when you pass them you give them a look that says
if you interfere with me or my kids
I'll kick the shite out of you.
Otherwise they'd have you hiding
Shergar's head in your chest of drawers.
This place is no great shakes to live in
but it's all we've got.
The dealers call it Bastards Bush.

I say to the kids, don't look at anything
on the way down those stairs;
the kids say to me like parrots,
we didn't look at anything mam,
we didn't look at the needles
or the shit or the broken glass.

Sometimes when I'm safe in my own flat
with all the locks and bolts on
I forget to take off the tiger skin.
The kids say, Mammy why are you cross again today?

## 2 *Food Patrol*

The kids want the food they see on telly.
I say telly isn't real,
when the ads are on I turn the telly off,
mind you it's wearing me out.
Tanya says mammies on the telly are nicer than me
even though she's only four
I feel hurt, I know I'm too hard on them.
I have to watch the food,
I'm on food patrol
and when they bring their friends in
I have to say spare the bread,
it kills me to have to say that to them.
it makes me feel mean.

I'm a Stretcher.
I can stretch things,
I crumble up one and a half Weetabix
and pretend they are getting two;
I add water to the milk,
they never know.
I never seem to say anything but
who was at the fridge
and who drank the last drop of milk,
I hate myself for it.

My neighbour and me meet every Friday night
we go shopping for bargains together,
we save pennies here and there
on overripe fruit and dodgy vegetables
after sell by date stuff.
We hang around the shops until closing time.
If there are any cooked chickens left
we get them at half price.
Our Dylan says our Saturday dinners
are nicer than our Sunday dinners;
we have chicken on Saturday
and soup on Sunday.
He says his friend Billy has roast on Sunday.
I say he's a liar, I bite my lip.


## 3 *If Looks Could kill*

We all hate the moneylenders
but we need them for the Communion gear and that

it's the only time our families get together, barring funerals,
and I wouldn't give to show
that my girls won't look their best
even if I'm paying for it for two years.
One day Catherine from the corner house said,
I suppose the moneylenders have to live too.
We just looked at her.


4 *The Clinic*

I went up for help
with the shoes and uniforms,
that sort of thing.
The woman at the hatch was a right fuckin wagon,
she said I was in the wrong place.
It took me two buses to get there.
I asked her where was the right place.
Try the Vincent de Paul, she said.
When I got outside
I cried with rage.


5 *Christmas*

Two weeks before and two weeks after Christmas
I don't give the bill boys anything,
I stock up for the Christmas.
Any money I have goes on things for the kids.
I make sure they have a good Christmas,
we even have Christmas cake.
The funny thing is the kids don't like Christmas cake.

January and February are very bleak.
I owe everyone and they are not shy about telling me.
My nerves always get the better of me,
the doctor says I should take something
to calm me down, I'm highly strung.
When a car pulls up with a zero zero number plate
I know its someone looking for money.

I say to the doctor I'd rather live on my nerves
than take anything, then by early February
I go back and ask him for something,
something small to tide me over.

## 6 *Queuing*

You think queuing for food is bad
but queuing for a hospital appointment is worse,
at least you know what a loaf of bread is,
you don't know what they are saying up here –
they look down on you like you were shit,
they use another language,
a keep them guessing language,
a language never heard up our side
and I've heard some choice language believe you me.
They might be educated
but they're just as intimidating as the pushers.
You go in feeling bad,
you come out feeling worse.


## 7 *If I Won the Lotto*

If I won the Lotto
I'd get a headstone for Anto's grave.
He died young,
he didn't just burn the candle at both ends,
he ate the candle.
I wouldn't say it was the drink killed him
but it wasn't the milk either.
He was a good father though,
the kids loved him.

When he died the neighbours made a collection.
A good neighbour round here
is when they know every detail about you
and they still like you.
They like me more than I like me
'cos I don't like me at all.

I'd probably take the kids to Blackpool
I saw it on Coronation Street once
it had lots of rides and games for the kids.
I'd buy them new toothbrushes
they have the same ones for years.

I'd buy lampshades for all the bulbs,
it's just one of those things
you put on the back boiler like a piano
or a Triton shower.
Lampshades were never a priority
in this house.

# THROW IN THE VOWELS

(2005)

# Ambrose Had A Big Heart

*ad majorem Dei gloriam*

Martin de Porres
got the Connell family everything.
He nodded his lovely head
in thank-yous when a penny hit the spot.

When the grocery van
pulled into Byrne's yard
good neighbours were ready.
Voices ran into each other
up the galvanised roof
down the ears of barking dogs.
It was a great place for news.

Lu Lu Connell gave us Ambrose-talk
and we lapped it, like fried bread dipped in egg.
'Ambrose now mind you is going to work
amongst the poor in South Africa,
and it's all down to Blessed Martin.'
The Holy Ghost Fathers had some connection
but it was all Nebula Febulorem.

Lu Lu always bought sweet cake from the van.
Light sponge smothered in coconut
lemon swiss roll, madeira, simnel cake,
iced log, battenberg.
She said the cake went straight to the soul
and the tea went straight on the hips.

They say Ambrose had a smashing global outlook,
and vision when no one had vision.
When he could hardly walk
he was collecting for the black babies.

So it came as no great shock to us
when one pancake Tuesday word rose up the queue
that Ambrose got a black baby of his own
and he married her.
She was twelve and three quarters.

LuLu never told us this,
it was brought to the village
on the lips of a Jesuit
who had yella fever
and no belongings.
They flew him back
in a plane full of air-mail letters,
on a wing and a prayer.

# After Dinner Speaker

*Increased means and increased leisure are the civilisers of man*
DISRAELI

Galway's Business and Professional Women's club
would like me to be their guest speaker.
Silly old me wanted a fee.
I used that dirty word before
to the outgoing President of the club.

She fell into her crystal shop in shock.
Shortly after her fall
she looked into her crystal ball;
it said, fee fee over my dead body from me
and she retired to her prism with aplomb.

The incoming P of BPW Galway.
would like me to be their guest speaker.
I used the dirty word again.
Fee fee foo fum.
I'm such a silly cow,
don't I know that it has never been
BPW Galway policy to pay a fee to guest speakers.
What kind of Óinseach am I?
Their aim is to empower women
not to pay poets or piss artists.

The incoming P of BPW Galway
could much appreciate how I would expect a fee
under normal circumstances
but not from the BPW Galway
who God help us, and as everybody knows
haven't a Capo De Monte pot to piss in.

But all is not frost;
if I were to reconsider
and give a talk
and read my poems –
only for a short while mind
between dessert and coffee –
the incoming P of BPW Galway
assures me that she knows,
because she can feel it in her bowels
and in the bowels of the other
two hundred and fourteen members
that the BPW Galway,
would show their Gottya Gucci appreciation
and their rolled gold appreciation so much
when they applaud, that the roof would lift
off the Ardilaun House Hotel
where the beleaguered Business Women of Galway
have their meetings on the first Friday of every month.

# The Liberator

*When our feet hurt, we hurt all over*
SOCRATES

When Grettie from Grealish Town
soaked and clipped –
you talked.
You'd tell her things
you kept from the priest.

At first there were doubts
about this whippersnapper
who worked in the hat factory.
What would she know
about stubborn old nails?

But the toenail gang knew her unflappable touch.
She would tuck cotton wool soaked in antiseptic
under an untameable bucko and deliver him.

You'd feel nothing more than her coaxing gaze
calling for, more story, more story.

## Wasting Time

My father always said
I'd end up in The San,
wearing that excuse for a skirt.

He never told me that while I slept
Leviathan and his clique
would whisk me for a skite on the high seas.
They'd sly off before dawn
leaving me covered in salt.

When my father visited me
he brought up *The Sentinel*
so that I could read about the hoodlums
who got nicked for stealing
jeans from the jean factory.

When the tea trolley came round
the visitors left.
I longed for the tea trolley.
My father's weekly howl
took a wider geographical swipe
I hadn't the energy to bark.
I nearly always let him win.

'The fish you landed
is fearful enough of the shovel
but in fairness being out of work
and being in jail
are not the same thing at all,
look at Charles Manson,
look at The Yorkshire Ripper.

As for this place,
I wouldn't dance a gig about it,
hot dinners or no hot dinners.
My advice to you is,
give nosy parkers the slow drip,
don't tell them what you have,
tell them you have a bad cold.
A bad cold could be anything
from nettle rash to pneumonia.
TB will always be TB.'

# The Servers

Altered boys in Ireland
have no egos
not to mind altar egos.
They have been ground down
by power-filled priests
who play pain games
with their bones
their brittle bones.

These wolves sit in parlours
in millennium sitting-rooms
with tongue-tied mothers
who are proud their sons are serving God.
They take one spoon or two
and much more.

When the father comes home
she tells him the priest was here.
They are filled with joy.
Our boy on the altar,
our lamb on weekends away
with father meekly,
how lucky are we.

We are so proud,
we are taller when we walk,
when we are walking
we are really running,
running with God.

We are prouder than our neighbours
whose son only works on the farm god help us.
We are sorry for them but our son serves god.

Our son the lamb
is away for the weekend
with father good who is really gooder,
father nice who couldn't be nicer
with his smashing sheep's frock,
his innocent flock
his holy hand always out
asking for nothing
but his ring to be kissed.

# The Cover-up

SENTRY

We threw dice to find out which of us
vile-worms-of-the-earth
would give you the baddest news my lovely king.
When the dice landed, it had my name on it.
The pet name you put on me last calendar, lovely king.
The dice read 'Dingo Face'.


KING

'Go on then, bad news me.
Mind you, seeing your dingo face
is bad news enough for me.
Spit it out or I'll have your entrails
plaited and caramelised.'


SENTRY

Thank you for coaxing my tongue o king,
excuse my stutter and if my inner organs
give a public showing, give them the blind eye.
Put it down to nervous delight at your Grace's threats.
He, he, he wasn't half covered,
it was just a blanket of dust my king
no one could call it a burial,
there was a dash of wine sprinkled nearby.
Don't read libation into it,
some drunk could have fallen over his sandal strap,
that would explain it.

When the king found out who covered Polyneices,
nails and molars flew from his mouth –
a gold tooth hit the wall,
hot steam with a dank odour hissed from his undercarriage,
his hair was blazing, he was a whisker pale.
Tiresias, who never lies, slow-footed it
to where the king was bellowing.

Hear me king, the birds are kicking
the lard out of each other
making it rain gizzard fat,
every dog-o-the-street knows
I am an expert in
reading the gizzard fat.
Take my blind advice
and release her before it is too late.
After all, what did she do
but cover her brother's body,
to deny the vultures a lip-smacking afternoon.

But the king was a know-all
with egos in every pocket, and no brains.
He paid heed only when death dripped
from the vault down to his street
and into his son's room
and into his wife's room and beyond
and the dank odour was everywhere.
All he could do was sit there like a Fooleen
with his hands covering his face.

# My Lucky Number

Doctors three four and five said
they could knock those thoughts
out of me in eleven easy treatments.

Doctors one and two were dead-heads,
doctors three four and five
were in with a scream.

Doctors six seven and eight said
they could knock  those thoughts
out of me in ten treatments.

Doctors four five and six were nowhere
doctors six seven and eight were the men.

Doctor nine said
he could sizzle those thoughts
in nine riveting treatments,
on top of that he would throw in
a cup of sweet tea when I woke up.

Doctors six seven and eight were history,
doctor nine was mine.

Doctor seven started making
a holy show of himself, saying
he would throw in a mass bouquet.
It was good for seven days
from the thirtieth to the thirty-eight of December.
My intentions (however sick)
would be included at eleven o'clock mass
in the Cathedral of Our Lady Assumed into Heaven and Saint Nicholas.

Doctor ten said
he would rid me of my inclement thoughts forever
in four easy peasy treatments. No frills.

I chose doctor nine.
The sweet tea swung it for me
that and the fact that when out eyes met
on the lanky corridor
of my demented dreams
it sent shock waves up my spine.
Coupled with that
nine is my lucky number.

# Grandchildren

It's not just feasible at the moment
one daughter tells me.
What with Seamus still robbing banks
and ramming garda vans when he gets emotional
on a fish-free Friday in February.

Maybe the other daughter could deliver.
She thinks not, not at the moment anyway
while Thomas still has a few tattoos to get,
to cover any remaining signs that might link him
with the rest of us.

Just now a B52 bomber flies over
on its way from Shannon
to make a gulf in some nation's genealogy.

The shadow it places on all our notions is crystal clear
and for a split of a second helping
it juxtaposes the pecking order.
Now bank robbers and tattooers
have as much or as little standing
as popes and princes
and grandchildren become another lonely utterance
impossible to pronounce.

## Anto's Inferno

It wasn't until our Anto
got fourteen months
for borrowing other people's cars
from their driveways
and making an inferno out of them
so that he could show his uncles
what a big man he was,
then and only then did we realise
what an insatiable appetite he had.

After he was lockjawed
in The Joy for a few months
our house was like a banqueting hall
with all that extra food.
Going through that food
was like a journey through hell
heaven and purgatory.

Anto's friend, Liver Lips,
called round one day
to tell us one thing about Anto
I'll tell ya one thing about Anto
he has great taste, he never touched nothin'
'cept Beamers and Mercs
and if they hadn't alloy wheels
there was no way he'd entertain them.
He'd babysit the odd Saab
but only if she was a zero four job.

We miss Anto round the house,
only the other mornin'
before I did the shoppin'
I opened our fridge,
there was enough frozen pizza in it
to feed all Castle Park,
untouched and no takers
they were just sittin' there
like Beatrice, waitin' for the beck.

## The Real Mourners

My sisters and I always cry at funerals.
We take over the back seat
normally reserved for mothers,
who lose their sons
to crocodile wrestling or
head-kicking bouncers.

We don't have to know the deceased,
we only have to be in the same room as the coffin.
The eldest sister, known locally as No Flowers,
the youngest we call House Private,
the middle sister is Mary Ann.
We had another sister, Good Grief,
she had a thing about therapists,
we released her with love.

When the real mourners see us, they say,
'There they go again, those pretenders,
those town criers, lettin-on-grief-strickers.
What have they got to cry about?
Their sons' heads have never been kicked in
by bouncers from The King's Knuckle.
More in their line to go home
and wash the children they have left.

They don't know the meaning of sadness
they have never lost anything in their lives
except maybe the odd stone off the hips
an ill-fitting shoe, or a dry cleaning ticket.
They'll wake the dead with that howling.'

But the real mourners
didn't read the morning papers,
otherwise they would know
the sisters are crying in advance
of the anorexic reaper's knock
and when that knock comes
they will have no tears left.
They will stand in the front of churches,
Ogham stones in dark coats and sunglasses.

# Fugued

My lovely brother cleans windows.
He likes to talk shop,
he likes to talk glass.
He can tell a lot about people
by the state of their windows.

Once I tried to change his chosen subject.
He warned me of the dangers of such sedition.
Stick to window cleaning
where you can see your reflection
and know exactly where you are.

He had contacts who knew where they were,
then one Saturday the Earth wobbled on its axis,
they were left lost at the side of a ditch looking for answers.
One no-hoper was looking for toast.

This visionary is different,
he knows exactly where he's not,
and when he's not up a ladder
he's not up a ladder.
Not knowing where he's not is foolproof
not knowing where he is another story.
He never works Saturdays.

He sees himself in the windows he cleans,
he never grows older,
he looks the same as he did
before the last currency change.
And as for lost, he'd tell you straight,
it has nothing going for it
it's only a word with a contrary O
that buckles like a window cleaner's dream.

\* \* \*

# Janus

Everyone's loneliness is following me around,
everywhere I go it's there waiting.
I tried the beach today
usually a safe haven –
but it was there and it only had eyes for me.

I slip in and out of
the heavy overcoat of it,
sometimes it weighs me down,
other times it weighs me down as well.

I tried to out-piebald it the other day
heading for the January sales,
wearing my Springer Spaniel shoes,
when I wear them I sing arias.

But not this time dog feet:
half price became full price,
twenty per cent off became twenty per cent more,
my cantata was sold from under my nose
to the highest bidder with the heaviest coat.
I was Philomela and my heart went out to myself.

I'm gagging for the stretch they talk about
at bus stops and doorsteps,
the long giraffe stretch in the evenings
when this beast of suburbia
will glide like Thetis into the sea.

# The Doppelgänger

In Portalonely with the new stockings,
the River Island skirt, she waited.
She drank, she door-watched,
any minute now he would stroll in,
half eight no sign.

The bouncers –
members of Mensa to a man –
reckoned she was on the game.
She must have got the pub name wrong,
half nine no sign.

He'll be caught in traffic, that'll be it –
she fixed her skirt, she watched the door.
The bouncers were cocksure –
bouncers always know a whore –
half ten no sign.

Not a bad pair of pins, said clever dick number one.
I'll be in there by midnight, said his brother the twin.
Their doppelgänger Loki was cleverer still.

Loki Kelly, interweaver people pleaser,
he didn't just knit, he crocheted,
he turned a cliché into a scream
when he looked in the mirror.
Elvis looked out at him,
when he looked in his wife
he saw Costa-Del-Empty,
no sea no sand,
half eleven no sign.

Loki's middle name was Portamento,
this gave him leverage and lip,
he knew about sideswipes and slips,
he could clematis, he could climb.

In Portalonely with the new stockings –
minutes to midnight no sign.
The mischief-maker was throwing shapes.
I'm Loki, I spark in bolts, I hurl in mine,
grey areas I can shade, black areas I can hide.
I've got the perfect potion, all you need is the rhyme.

# Perdition

From the word go he went
and he never came back.
She watched and waited
while the signals grew ill-bred
and vague.

Times before he went
he didn't exactly stay,
he hovered on her linear sill,
odd times blocking the rain,
odder times blocking the light.

He was the well-built phantasm
with cars and coats and clichés.
She fell into the clichés,
the cars were out of bounds,
the coats didn't fit.

Still, she bought into the daydream
of a journey for two,
a field trip to Phobos,
a wet day in Coole Park.

When she couldn't see him
she thought she saw him,
he'd fade, she'd rescue,
he was back in her thoughts,
they all had high voltage,
needle-pricks to the heart.

# Throw in the Vowels

Fling odd bouquets from the tip of your tongue;
say to him, Adonis pet, you have golden beryls
like those on the brown bull of Cooley.

Be careful not to overdo it;
never use hung-like-a-hippo comparisons
lest he question your sincerity.
Look deep in his eyes for answers,
if the whites are favourable see how matters stand.

If he still shows gamey eye after he pleasures you much,
give him slap on bare backside.
If glint still persists give him slap with bat,
not baseball bat but flat bat, no call to oil bat
with oil of eucalyptus or any other concoction.

If there was a night last week
he did not gratify then he owes you for that.
No need to broadcast this tidbit
when his mother and nine sisters are in earshot.
Still, you have to be compensated for off nights
or under the weather nights, think bat think bull.

If his memento mori has a hungdog look about it
make him talk about other lovers,
that will spur him on, they love to boast,
allow him eight hefty perjuries.

If he does not gratify three nights in a row
give him small member talk,
no need to stretch it past infinity,
four or five small-member-minutes will do.
After that lift his spirits,
tell him altar in the garden story,
tell him altar in the garden with his name on it story,
it always works.

When the intense thing is happening
allow him to shout six or seven obscenities,
make it a condition that the obscenities have no vowels.
If a hungdog focus comes back on the mori
hurl in a fistful of vowels.

Remind him of your nobility the next time he gets cocky.
Say to him, mark the night the intense thing was happening
and you couldn't cut it and I tossed in a few buckshee vowels,
'member that my love?


## They Had No Song


It had all the hallmarks
of something passionate.
It looked real, it sounded real
but in the end as in the beginning
it was nothing more than the dream team
playacting the big roll, skirting on the outside of devotion,
on the rim of lit cities, periphery smiffphery
outside Christmases, inside themselves,
making things bigger, multiplying when adding would do.

Phones didn't help, too many pauses,
one didn't know whether the other was cooing or coming,
e-mails were worse more periphery smiffphery,
all cryptic and vague, nothing ventured nothing stained,
no stain no gain, no Sunday afternoons to fuck in,
no long weekends made longer by lingus kissus,
no bulgaricus on each other's bad habits,
no data on his'n'her Incubus or Succubus,
no special place to eat, no favourite colour,
except they both got the blues on a regular basis.

Absolutely no pets,
there was talk of a goldfish,
Hades for a boy, Fugue for a girl,
the upkeep and the fungus
forget that, forget birthdays,
no middle names no nicknames
no Casablanca, they had no song.

# Dry-mouthed and Melancholy

Her punishment, her lizard tongue:
it had the power to knock seagulls sideways,
she was big mouth honest,
couldn't keep anything in
on the other foot he was keep it all closed up,
clam tart up to his lovely heart.

His punishment, he withheld love
with Fort Knox ferocity.
Unlike Orpheus he didn't look back out of love,
he just didn't look back.

The spectre that led them was on Valium and Red Bull.
They were always lost; she was more lost than him
because Harry Hope hung round her
with an oxygen tent and credit for her mobile phone,
making mischief out of her juvenile jaunts
through the ventricles that were not yet clogged
with psychobabble and maybes.

She couldn't find her knickers,
he couldn't find his Merc,
he couldn't find her knickers either
even though she was wearing them on her head.
It was a sad scenario of wrong direction
and very crossroads that lead nowhere.

She told the one in the shadows how shady he was
and how his half-truths only fed her half the time
and the puzzlement was she loved the one in the shadows.
From the start it was a painful love,
all mangled like the handlebar sculptures
that passes for art at roundabouts in Irish towns.

There was no going back, no going forward,
no French kissing, no Irish kissing, no pleasure of any sort
except the odd time he appeared in her dreams
proffering nine talking penises.
The penises gave back cheek and she loved it,
in the dream she licks her lips
but when she woke up she was dry-mouthed and melancholy.
She swore she must give up the smokes,
she gave up dreaming instead.

# Nikita

Nikita,
you have left me
on this plinth of isolation
for three hundred years.
My swan's neck stretching
for that chink of light
that never comes.

Nikita,
be unkind to me if you like
only for Christ's sake
be something to me.

Nikita,
a kind word
or an unkind word
could last for weeks or months,
try one.

Nikita,
I hear your keys rattle from outside,
that sound means something,
multiply it.

Nikita,
do you ever think
how deafening it is for me
to be on the receiving end
of your long silences.

Nikita,
when you don't anything me
for as long as you don't
it gives me hope,
unreal hope.

# Terminus

There was no acoustic
in their walk or talk,
not even a gate-swing creak
in their half rhyme
that held no rhythm
and went with nothing.

They didn't match,
they didn't fit,
still they chiselled away
below the surface
for something faint or familiar
that might unite them.

It never happened,
it never will.

\* \* \*

# His i's Were Empty

The only thing I liked
about my father
was his handwriting.

His n's were slender and mean,
they had big-city-never-seen
written all over them.

His r's were turned in secret-keepers,
they stole or owed nothing
to chance or design.

His n's were nowhere now
but they had travelled
through continents
of isolation and sting.

His m's were memorable,
his mother was free,
she died before she could
wing him a lullaby.
His m's now mine to take or leave,
I took a left and lost.

The spines of his k's
were sentinel straight –
once teddy-boy wise
now corner-men lonely.
The watchers of history,
the warmers of stone.

His g's were fractured and cross,
snarling like the Leitir Móir mongrels
at the cheating half-days of winter.

His eyes were empty,
except for that gulf of longing
that gaped around syllables,
making contact a cavity
language never reached.

# The Hedger

In Bally Brit
when my father cut the hedge
he whistled and from time to time
he fixed his cap.
Cutting the hedge was a big job
that only a father could do
he was unflappable then
well able for the stillness
that latched onto him.

When the border was out of reach
a kitchen chair came in handy,
as he stood on the chair
to pare the unreachable
the clippers were turned backwards,
no problem for the hedger
who could clip six inches off your smile
with a mere half sentence.
Later, that chair would be used
for tired elbows to lean against
while we prayed
for the grace of a happy death.

As he cut,
I gaped from the hem of the barrel
that coaxed rainwater
down a gutter,
for washing faces
and brothers' shirts.

He whistled
and from time to time
the hedger fixed his cap.
Little did we know
that when we'd reckon days and juggle months
we'd border on a territory much clipped,
our resentments in a row,
our contentment out of reach,
our choler cropped.

## Loquacia L. Spake

Lo Lo Spake
was on the early train
from Galway to Dublin
one crisp crisp morning in May.

She was two seats behind me,
her mobile phone rang and rang.
I'm on the train, she yells to Garrulla.
She laughs an awful lot of laugh,
a laugh that carries a harpy inflection,
a few wasps fiddling in the throat thrown in.

'Not a problem' and 'cheers'
her mantra to Garrulla
in a pitch pitch pitch
that wasn't nice and wasn't real.

I was bumble
I was bumble
I was bitch bitch bee
I was me, she was she.

She saw *Eastenders* last night
and it was real, it had appeal
and it was 'brill' she told Garrrrr
she told me.

She missed the first half of *Coronation Street*
because her sister 'Silent Night'
wanted to know what happened on *Eastenders*
and she had to give her a blow blow
and all that blah blah
with harpies and wasps scratching round the windpipe,
it was never going to be
all sponge cake round the Ricky Ricky Lake.

I was slaughterous with information
I was ashen with vexation
I was more *tion tion* than Rin Tin Tin
I was Anna Karenina
I was Kermit the dog.

Lo Lo is going to Dublin for the sales, ya ya,
she was out three nights at the weekend, ba ba.
She wore the grey top on Friday night,
it wasn't great with the trousers with the glitter,
that she got in London in Feb, ya ya,
when she went over to see *Riverdance*
which was 'brill'
but she got away with it
because of her height, ba ba.

On Saturday night
she wore the black top
with the loop-neck and the hipsters
she got for a song in A-Wear last Juno.

We've reached Athlone,
I'm not alone
I've got Lo Lo L. Spake
who spoke and spoke
and Garrulla who would speak and speak
if only she would, if only she could.

I was bumble
I was bumble
I was bitch bitch bee
I was me, she was she.

# Rolled-up Race Card Days

*(for my brother Jose)*


When our aunts arrived from Maree
carrying car loads of cousins and laughter
we spilled out onto the front garden.
Sunday aftermoons seemed endless then
and you were younger.

Your strenuous efforts against going to school
were never brought up on these happy occasions.
But your struggle against school was ongoing
whether the cause was personality or principle,
you just didn't want to go, and you often didn't.

A childhood of shadows and light
of listening to older people talk,
where Martin de Porres was on night duty
and Saint Jude did the daytime watch.
The Clancy Brothers were a feature
so was Fats Domino
echoes of Marty Robbins,
Péigí Lítirmore was always in the wings,
maybe not your choice
but it was your diet and ours
and it was real
like the mummers
like the wran the wran
like the candles we lit on small Christmas
charting which of us would live the longest.

Other things lodge in the memory
like news that Grandad was slack,
or Rebel, the dog everyone loved,
or the Honda 50 and its sanguine history,
picking hazelnuts, blackberry-picking,
cold tea for sore eyes,
going to Flynn's in Wood Quay,
going to the Poor Clares,
going to the well,
going to hell if we didn't watch it.
The world was edging nearer chaos
because God spent all his time watching the Higgins's.

In a dream
mother said to tell you she was proud, very proud.
And as for us
we were proud long before this
when your innocence was plaited with ours in Bally Brit.
Where Patrick Craven's whistling
was all the security we needed for a good night's sleep.
In Winnie's you played cards with the big lads.
In T-Silk's caravan we watched our first films
and when televison did come
we watched it with you through O'Connors' window.

Race days were special.
Ham sandwiches with mustard days.
Parking cars for Mrs Grogan for a half a crown
using a rolled-up race card to guide them in
up Lawlers.
You liked the horses then
and rumour has it
you like them now.

You were fashioned by these things
but you were fueled by fire and a desire to succeed
and you did. Your vision was clear.
You made a difference
a staggering difference.
That's why you're here.

*June 27th 2003: to celebrate the conferring of an Honorary Doctorate on our brother Joe.*

# The World Is Getting Smaller

I text our Heather
on the Mekong Delta.
I asked her had she any news.
She texted back:
Becks got loose but he didn't get far
and would I tape Coronation street for her.

My sister and I love the central heating,
we talk about it ever chance we get
except when she talks about
*Riverdance* going to China.
If her legs were good she'd be a dancer.
She'd dance in Latvia or Estonia.
She asks me if I am warm,
I say are you warm?
I asked you first she says.

My brother moved back
to the mobile home near the motorway.
I feel sorry for him,
he feels even sorrier for me.
he pities me sitting in coffee shops
writing poems that nobody reads.
I pitied him first

He says, don't piticise what you can't understand.

The papers are full of Falluja,
my other sister whose legs are good
wants to go to Slovenia or Slovakia
not to dance but to language,
the Kelly twins are going on the Ho Chi Minh Trail,
thanks to the credit union
they'll bring me back a stick of rock.

A writer I know wrote poems about Tibet
but he never left town.
Tibet came to him in books and dreams.
Bob Dylan came to Galway in a limousine.

# No Chance Encounters

*(in memory of our brother Tony)*

> *The past is not dead*
> *it is not even past*
> WILLIAM FAULKNER

No hope now of a serendipitous encounter
with you in Shop Street or the Eyre Square Centre.
Yourself and Joan strolling with ease
through the streets of the town that you loved.
It seemed strange to always bump into you
in the same part of town.

You didn't believe in coincidence or the chance encounter
or the curious way the cards sometimes fell
hurtling people on journeys they hadn't set out on.
What fate ordained was no puzzlement to you.

After we'd reply to your greeting, you'd always say:
But how are you really?
You'd smile that knowing smile
that suggested you knew something we didn't.
You knew us well.

This is how we knew you.
Champion of your brothers in Brier Hill School,
learner of languages, hugger of sisters,
philosopher, Johnny Casher, jazz devotee,
lover of Lightnin' Hopkins Blues,
of Billie Holiday, of Ella Fitzgerald.
Blues lover who rarely got the blues.

Nothing surprised you, nothing fazed you,
you were as much at home in the streets of Galway
as you were in the desert with the Bedouins.
With much ease you would spend hours
sitting, listening, learning,
always fearless because you were with friends.

While we waited for you to come home for the last time
we plucked stories from acute memories
that needed no prompting.
We delved into boxes of photographs
trying to find the last one taken of you.

The photographs brought more memories:
you in Bally Brit where you grew up,
you in Maree with Carmel,
you in the Congo, you in the Holy Land,
you were fearless long before this.

You with Joan, you with Siobhán, you with Nicole,
you loved them together
and you loved them separately.
Trips to Roundstone,
trips to Morans of the Weir,
lover of photography, cigar smoker,
Nicole didn't know how much she'd miss
the smell of those cigars.

You had a keen interest in Irish history, world history,
you loved debate, you'd argue with the devil.
You had fluent Arabic,
you taught yourself German.
Later you learned how to text,
how early and how often
your daughters have the inside story.
Siobhán has your last text,
a text to treasure.

You with us at Auntie Kathleen's funeral,
a strange time for taking photographs
but family get-togethers were hard to surpass,
even the sad ones were happy ones in the end.

How could we forget that time in your house
after Father's funeral
when Mary did the writhing actions
to make us reckon Crocodile Dundee
was the film she had in mind?
When it was your turn to beguile us
no one could match your meticulous by heart rendition
of dangerous Dan McGrew.
A pause in the skylarking
gave you the leeway to baffle us further
with sidekick Sam McGee.

Tony Higgins, soothsayer, prayer sayer,
holy man, funny man, brother, father, husband, friend.
You said there are no coincidences, no chance encounters
our destiny is predetermined,
no crystal-gazing for you, no Mystic Meg.

We will commemorate you for this
and for the limitless insights you have given us.
We will lay you to rest in sadness,
afterwards we will celebrate your life –
the only way we know how,
and the way we know you would love
with libation and song.

# That Shower

My neighbours are a pair of good-looking fools,
they drill and drill,
not just now and again
but then and now and then again,
and often when I'm in,
I'm oftener in.

I've had this faint dash of piss for perfume
since the waterworks slowed down.
That doesn't stop me hammering
the free travel pass ever chance I get.
I skite off some Friday nights
to a B and B that's over a shop.
I have a shower'n'all in the room.
I nearly got one in at home once but I decided against it,
no point in wasting all that water,
best decision I ever made.
The pair of good-looking fools
have a shower and a piano –
they never use either.

They have a Rotweiler called Gripper –
he ate a child's leg once
and they never put him down,
in fact they put him up
on the front window for all to see,
the Halloweeners speed up
when they see that piano.

I like to go to Newry for the night
but you have to change the money over,
anyone would think you were in another country.
I wish my neighbours were in another country.

When they don't drill and drill
they shout and shout,
not just now and again
but then and now and then again,
often when I'm out,
I'm often out
I'm oftener in.

I buy two magazines for the B and B,
not that I like magazines,
only if the film on the telly is no good,
and if Humphrey Bogart isn't in it
it's usually no good.

I can stomach Frank Sumatra for a while
but he can't act for nuts.
The good-looking fool calls his wife a bucket a-piss –
he's no rosebush himself
to be calling anyone a bucket-a-piss.
The magazines will bring the sleep on,
not that they're good, in fact they're bad,
that's why it's easier to sleep than to read them.

I'd love to show Humphrey the shower in this place.
Another thing, next door calls his wife is a poxy-cunt,
that's a regular two-liner,
mind you I like the sound of that.
I think about all the Luckies Humphrey smokes,
I think about him playing next door's piano.
I think about his waterworks.

# Return to Sender

*One woman against the letter of the law*
IRISH TIMES, 18 DECEMBER 2004

(Brid Cummins was found dead in bed
on the day she was due for eviction, 6 DECEMBER 2004)


Our acting city manager
never stops acting.
he never stops playacting.
He's a rule-book carrier.
he letter-of-the-laws it.
he jaw-jaws it.
He praises and praises,
his full of humanity staff,
his staff who gush with kindness,
his staff who sing while they work,
his staff who say, good morning,
how may I help you?
Free from blame all the same,
a councillor said, exonerated,
they are all exonerated,
staff exonerated he said it again.
Another councillor said policy
policy, policy, we have to carry out council policy.
Galway City Council policy.
We have to letter-of the-law-it,
we have to jaw-jaw it.

Good staff, lovely staff,
full of humanity staff,
gush when we walk staff,
gush when we talk staff.
Staff exonerated, all exonerated.
Policy policy, letter of the law, all jaw-jaw.

Clever letter-writing member of humanity staff
writes great letter bereft of hope,
sends great letter bereft of hope
to emergency housing authority 'Cope'
telling Cope to spare the hope this Christmas.

Don't re-house her
when we evict her,
the clever letter writer wrote
in a clever letter sent to Cope.
A clever letter bereft of hope.

She answers back,
she calls back.
She's a trouble-maker.
She's riddled with anti social behaviour,
she claims a back injury,
she's always looking for repairs,
and if it's not repairs it's a transfer.
She's taking legal action against us.
She pisses us off
and us dribbling with humanity.
we gush when we walk.
we gush when we talk.
we are exonerated.
A councillor said so,
exonerated, staff exonerated,
we were carrying out council policy,
Galway City Council policy.

Our acting city manager,
our playacting city manager,
playacts on our behalf.
He has a duty to protect his staff.
He has a duty to protect his back.
He knows how kind we are
all year round
but especially at Christmas.